successful
home
repair

successful
home
repair

When *Not* to Call the Contractor

Gary Paulsen

With illustrations by
Ruth Wright

Structures Publishing Company
Farmington, Michigan

Manufactured in the United States of America

Edited by Shirley M. Horowitz

Book design by Carey Jean Ferchland

Cover photos by Ann Arbor Photographic, Inc.

Current Printing (last digit)
10 9 8 7 6 5 4 3 2 1

Structures Publishing Co.
Box 1002, Farmington, Mich. 48024

Library of Congress Cataloging in Publication Data

Paulsen, Gary.
    Successful home repair.

    Includes index.
    1. Dwellings—Maintenance and repair—Amateurs' manual
manuals.   I. Title.
TH4817.3.P38   643'.7   78-9107
ISBN 0-912336-69-2
ISBN 0-912336-70-6 pbk.

contents

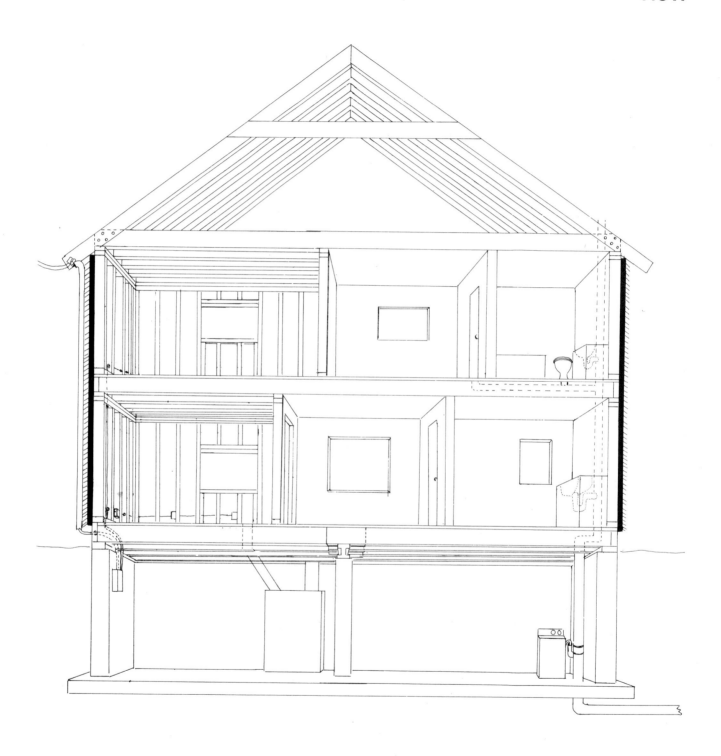

6

avoiding repair

Perhaps the greatest irony in any discussion of home repair—for all aspects of the home—is that the best home repair is the one you didn't have to make. Barring natural disasters and accidents, a major portion of all home repairs needn't have happened in the first place.

It could easily be said that most problems around the home which require repair or replacement are caused by sheer neglect. This neglect is not purposeful. It often arises from ignorance more than anything else—an ignorance perpetuated a great deal by unscrupulous contractors—but is nonetheless devastating.

Consider a small leak in a roof. It can be easily fixed, as will be discussed in specific detail later, usually with a bit of tar or mastic. The job can take less than five minutes and cost under a dollar.

But if the leak is allowed to develop and grow, the ensuing damp-damage to the attic and roof trusses (especially if a rot pattern appears) can be nearly catastrophic. It's quite possible that a few months neglect can cause major roof damage over an extended period. If the rot goes into the rafters it might well require roof replacement, which is virtually as expensive as building new.

So before getting down to specifics, here is a general chapter on prevention of major repairs.

Knowing Your Home

Usually, when presenting methods of repair prevention, the term *maintenance* is brought in. And to be sure, a thorough program of maintenance can do unbelievable amounts of good when it comes to avoiding problems. Indeed, it might be said that maintenance is the key to all problems; some suggested methods of maintenance will be examined shortly.

But there is another, more subtle aspect to home problems; this aspect deserves study. It revolves around the "feeling" of the home, or might be called the tuning of the house. It is what one architect has described as "...the life force of the dwelling."

Whatever you choose to call it, the way the house "feels" to you, the person who has to live in it, can have a measurable effect on the when and/or how of home repair.

A home heating system that is ill designed for your specific needs (for instance, inadequate in those areas where you want heat, or too much for comfort) can breed a kind of mental distaste—a subtle almost-anger that can and most often will cause repair problems because you may overload the system working it too hard, or imbalance it to try to make it fit your needs by constantly changing temperature settings, or neglect the whole thing because in a hidden part of your mind you resent it.

It is not the purpose of this book to stress architectural evaluation of dwellings, nor to cover extensive remodeling. But in a very definite way this consideration, which controls the way the house feels to you, should be taken into account as part of a home repair program. If some part of the house does not suit your needs, think about changing it, lest it become a repair problem down the road.

Maintenance

On a more practical level, the process of preventive repair centers on maintenance, as previously mentioned.

Here again there is a tendency to hit a superficial level and let it go. The classic illustration of this tendency to skip over important items is the forced air heating system. Promptly each late summer or fall most people replace the input air filters. Then they set their thermostats and forget the heating system for the rest of the winter.

While it is true that replacing the filters is vital—it can save much money in heating bills and ease the work of the blower—it is only the tip of the iceberg when it comes to preventive maintenance. True heating system maintenance should take an entire day, cover not just the filters but the blower motor, duct system, chimney (all will be covered shortly) so that when you're finished, you're actually *done* and you don't have to worry. (As for filters, many people in dirty or dusty climes change them each month and save money doing it, the way fuel prices are climbing.)

The thing to remember is that P.M. (preventive maintenance), to be effective, must be comprehensive and done in sufficient depth to catch any and all trouble spots in the house. For this reason the worst approach is the haphazard one. And the best way to attack the complications of a thorough maintenance system is to mimic the pros of P.M.—the airlines.

Nothing in air travel is left to chance or memory. Everything from the food to the wheels is logged and charted, and nowhere does this comprehensive listing get as detailed as in the P.M. methods. Even brake drums have their own data log systems, as well as the tires—*nothing* is left to chance. Nothing is left uninvestigated.

Of course home maintenance isn't always the life or death situation that commercial airlines represent, but it can be critical just the same. Keeping a maintenance log system on your home can mean large savings in both money and headaches. With home prices and all associated fees rising at their current astronomical rates a good maintenance system could easily save thousands of dollars.

The word to note is "*complete* maintenance system." Don't just run out and get a clipboard and tablet and scribble a blurb about the heater now and again. Be thorough. In fact you might consider your house as a plane—a main structure with several smaller support systems—and buy several clipboards, one for each system. Then pick a wall in the basement or other out-of-the-way place, slap up a piece of pegboard with hooks or drive in enough nails to take all the clipboards, label the nails with the proper names and leave plenty of spare room because there will be other clipboards added as time goes on.

A basic starting list of different systems to log follows. (Note: it is meant to be suggestive only and if you have other systems be sure to add them; better too many than not enough.) Each of the maintenance charts will be covered in detail shortly; this list merely estimates how many clipboards to buy initially.

Main house;

Heating and air conditioning system;

Plumbing system;

Roof and attic;

Electrical system;

Exterior wall (and siding);

Window (including storms and screens);
   Door (including storms and screens);

Interior wall and ceiling;

Floor (and floor covering)—which can also include stairways;

Foundation and basement—to include waterproofing, and the floor joists overhead if they are visible;

Appliances—to encompass dishwashers, clothes washers and driers, kitchen stove, ovens (including microwave), all major appliances in the home;

Supplementary, to include any and all systems or structures not already covered.

It is, as might be expected, a substantial amount of work to formulate the logs. But once they are done and copied out at the local library or wherever you can find a copier, the work eases out and the jobs take on order.

As for specific breakdowns for the various logs, following are some suggested formats which might help.

For the Main House Log, you simply want a list of the other log systems to maintain order, and keep a running tally of dates checked, as per the sample below:

MAIN HOUSE LOG

Unit	Date Checked	Remarks
Heating system	Jan.	Filter changed.
Plumbing system	Feb.	Damp around commode (see plumbing log for details).
Roof and Attic	Mar.	Small leak in N/W corner (see roof log for details).

And so on. Just a way to keep track of keeping track, to minimize the confusion. It is in getting down to the individual lists where comprehensiveness pays off. Following are several suggested logs and their application—again, shown as an illustration only. Don't limit yourself. Also, don't ignore manufacturer's information booklets, especially for appliances and heating- or air-conditioning systems. Often they furnish a complete maintenance list which you simply have to copy. And finally, remember that the main thrust of the maintenance logs is to stop expensive repairs before they happen, so it's better to be too picky than to miss something.

HEATING SYSTEM LOG

Item Checked	Date	Remarks
Filter	Aug.	Put in new filter.
Ducting	Aug.	Cleaned dust and cobwebs.
Motor	Sept.	Oiled bearings.
Burners	Sept.	O.K.
Pilot system	Sept.	O.K.
Pipes (for hot water)	Sept.	Slight dampness; keep watching.
Boiler (hot water)	Sept.	O.K.

And so forth. The important part of the list is to keep a running maintenance comment so that if something starts to go bad it will show. For example, the dampness around the pipes in the hot water system might be, probably is, simply condensation that will dry off. But it also might be a pinpoint leak which if watched could be stopped before it develops further.

Also, remember that the list is for you, personally, so don't worry if it's professional-sounding or not. As long as it works for you, that's the main thing. Then, too, write everything down whether or not it seems important at the time. In the heating system log, as an example, the cleaning of dust and cobwebs from around the ducts is noted not simply because it eliminates a fire danger (which it does); by noting the date it is possible to see how fast the dust builds and know if you should change your filter more frequently.

If in your plumbing log, for instance, you note that a drain is draining slowly when checked, you have two options. You can wait until it plugs completely and either call a plumber or use a snake to clear it out, or you can try some of the drain cleaning agents in the meantime and perhaps reopen it before it becomes plugged.

Or if a faucet washer leaks and allows a small drip, you can replace it before the drip becomes a torrent or wears away the surface below.

ELECTRICAL LOG

Item Checked	Date	Remarks
Visible wiring (in basement, etc.)		Inspected for fraying, burned spots.
Circuit breaker box (or fuse box)		Dirt, dust, burned spots.
Outlets and switches		Clean and working properly.
Light fixtures		Replace burned out bulbs, check wires, clean.
Power lines into house		Clear of branches and drains.
Loading		Check any circuit that pops breakers or blows fuses.

A cautionary thought: *all* electrical items should be considered potentially dangerous. For that reason any inspection of electrical wires should be done as carefully as possible—paying attention to safety logic and rules laid down in the chapter on electrical repairs. If you aren't comfortable enough with electrical work to do a good job, stay away from it.

ROOF AND GUTTER LOG

Item Checked	Date	Remarks
Visible roof		Clean, not decomposing.
Attic		No rot, no dampness, good insulation.
Gutters		Clear, open, non-rusted or jammed.
Soffit; eaves		No rot, loose or hanging soffit material.
Branches		Not scraping through roofing material.

It isn't necessary to list all the logs in detail, by now you will have recognized the main point to be completeness combined with common sense.

Frequency of the checks is not as critical as being sure they get done. Also, it varies greatly with area, weather conditions, the type of dwelling, and material used in construction. Checking the roof once a year, for example, right before bad winter or rain weather, is probably more than ample to catch any and all problems. The floor only needs a check every year or so. Running one general maintenance check on each of the logs each year will probably do the job; it is certainly more than many home dwellers do. And by cycling the checks around the year it is possible to further reduce the labor to one small inspection each month, and so no hard work at all. Little enough work if it prevents calling the contractor.

chapter two

aging

Houses, as the saying goes, begin to get old the minute they're finished and moved into. Indeed, with the rapid workmanship and the still-green wood going into many houses due to increased demand, aging problems in houses are understandable.

The problems covered in this chapter are due directly to the aging process, due to all the materials getting older and the house settling over time.

Sagging

A general letting down over the years is to be expected, and presents no real problem. Some tiny cracks will appear in the plaster; now and then you'll hear a creak; some lines that should have been purely straight will have a slight curve, although a not-unpleasant curve. Nothing really bad will happen. That's just normal aging, and isn't all that important.

But now and then a piece of wood will let go, or the sagging of a house will cause the doors to work poorly, or jam the windows. This is when aging becomes a hazard and repair is necessary.

The first thing, of course, is to locate the center of the sag. That is not as difficult as it sounds. You go into the basement or crawlspace beneath the point where you first noticed the sag, and make a visual inspection. If a door frame upstairs, for instance, has been getting tighter and tighter to work, you go into the basement under that point and study the overhead.

The point of sag will show, visually, as the low point in a curve.

The trick is to get it to go back up, and again, it's really a very simple process.

You rent a five ton jack from the nearest rental agency, cut a 4 x 4 inch post off to use as a jacking member, and take a second piece to spread the load. Then you jack the house back up, as illustrated.

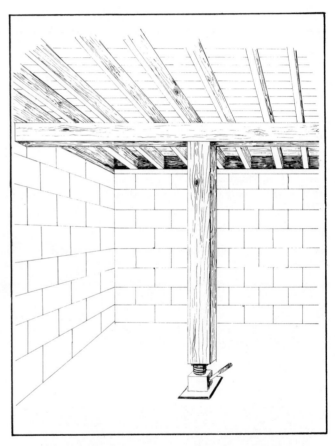

First jack the house up, just enough to take the sag out.

Go very slowly, just a hair at a time, to give all the boards time to catch up with this reverse movement; don't overdo it. The house will move easily, perhaps too easily, and there is a tendency to overcompensate.

When you have between half an inch and an inch of movement, stop! Leave everything as it is and go upstairs to see that the door or windows are working properly again. If so, don't go any further, because you will go too far and cause structural problems the other way. Be satisfied with what you've achieved.

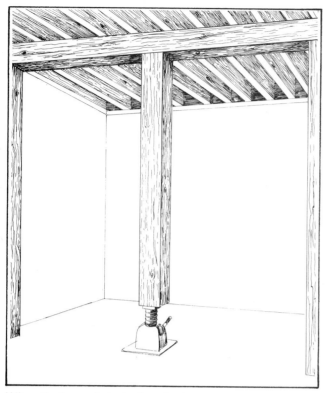

When the house is jacked on the 4x4 beam, put in two vertical supports to take the weight; then take the jack out.

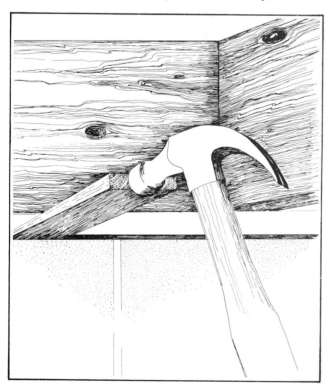

Drive the shingles in straight and hard. When they have moved the house up enough, cut them off flush with the wall and insulate the sill plate as shown.

Leave the jack holding the sagging section up, and build a support. Using 4 x 4 inch posts, as in the sketch, build a post-and-support-beam to hold the adjusted section up.

This post should rest on cement. If the basement has a cement floor, cut the vertical posts to rest on the cement and that will do it.

If the floor is earth, which might be the case in many older homes, buy two small slab-blocks—the kind that are solid and measure 8 x 16 x 4 inches thick—and use them for mini-footings for the vertical supports. Just put the post so it hits in the middle of the block on each end, and the two will hold up each end of the support beam.

With the beam in place, release the jack so the weight comes down on the support structure. Then go upstairs to see if the side effects are cured and the doors work properly.

If the corrected surface comes down too much, jack it back up and shim above the posts with shimming shingles between the post and support, as the sketch shows.

Note. If you intend occupying the area beneath the sag, using the place where the vertical posts come down, it is necessary to place the posts so they will be out of the way. One can go flush against the wall, obviously. But the other must be out there in the proposed room. If this is the case, place it either centrally, or where you propose putting a corner at some future date. This will save moving it later, which can be easily done.

Also, if the sag is in a corner of the house, which is usual in soft-soiled areas, the post support system is not necessary. Jack the corner up as with the central sag, but then simply jam shimming shingles back between the sill plate (the board that the floor joists are nailed to) and the top of the foundation wall. Pound the shingles in with a hammer, one every three or four inches, so they're driven in enough to take the load and then a little.

Then release the jack slowly, and check to make sure the side effects are gone.

The biggest danger in correcting sag is that the load will not be distributed over a wide enough area, so use a long 4 x 4 across the top. And be sure not to overdo it; don't, under any circumstances, jack it back up over an inch.

Shrinkage

Another problem due to aging is shrinkage. As wood becomes old and dries out, it shrinks.

Drive the fiberglass into the sillplate seam as hard as you can. Cut the insulation a little bigger than the space between the joists in order to stop all air leaks.

This causes noises, creaks, and a general opening of seams that might be considered unsightly. It will be especially noticeable in molding corners on the floor or ceiling, and in the finished carpentry work of exposed box beams and hairline cracks in plaster or drywall seams.

You can't make the wood come back to its original size (except sometimes in the case of floors, which will be discussed later), but you can compensate for the shrinkage to make it look better.

First, if the shrinkage has caused a pulling-apart of two boards, use a buffer board and try pounding them back together. Just a bit. This form of repair would work in such cases as a top door casing that lifts up and off the two vertical trim boards. Just tap it back down, not with massive blows but firm taps, and a buffer board between so the trim board doesn't get damaged by the hammer. This method would also work on an outside corner of molding, where the two mitered boards have moved apart, leaving a crack. Once again, just tap them back together.

On inside corners, or in other cases where hammering can't bring the boards back together, the repair is slightly more involved.

Wear rubber gloves and work wood filler into the crack with your thumb. Using premixed, precolored wood filler (get it as close to the right color as possible) will make the job easier. When the crack is filled, stain or paint to match if necessary. Be sure to work the filler completely back into the crack with your finger or thumb. If it only seals across the surface, and does not achieve any depth, it will crack open easily later.

Door shrinkage problems will be covered in the chapter on doors, but vertically sliding windows present particular problem when they become smaller. From left to right, the only effect is that they are slightly easier to slide up and down. But the shrinkage affecting them and allowing them to move back and forth can also cause them to wobble in the wind (resulting in curious thumping sounds) as well as let too much cold in and heat out.

To cure this you do nothing to the window itself. Instead, inspect the window and you will notice that on wooden windows there is a strip that goes up the side of the casing so the window can slide; it is simply nailed in with finishing nails.

Using a screwdriver and hammer, carefully remove the slider strip, poke out the nails, and renail it back against the window so that it is snug the full vertical distance the window moves. This will "tighten" up the whole assembly and minimize the problems caused by aging.

This same aging-shrinkage sometimes causes the glass to be loose in wooden-stopped windows—or in the old routed mullion kind. Repair procedures are essentially the same. Pull the stops carefully, one at a time, and move them closer to the glass and renail. Use a piece of cardboard or fiberboard to protect the glass from the hammer. If you do not feel up to pulling all the stops, and it is only a small wobble in the glass, you might try a thin, pressured-in bead of caulking—so little that it is practically invisible—all around the glass. Just squirt it in between the glass and then stop, being careful not to slop over, and it should take the wobble out.

Rot

Perhaps the most critical structural problem found in older homes is old-fashioned rot, also sometimes known as dry rot.

It will be found in attics and basements primarily, though it can show up anywhere. It starts with a blackening of the wood which eventually leads to the wood literally rotting and falling to pieces. To test for rot, probe and poke with your screwdriver. Soft, easy-to-penetrate spots mean trouble, as does easy splintering.

If your house has rot, and the rot is advanced and in structural areas such as rafters or floor joists, there is little you can do except replace the rotted member. Doing this is just exactly as difficult and messy as it sounds—not at all something for the amateur. The old member has to be ripped out, a new one cut and put in. It is terrible.

If, however, the rot is not greatly advanced and has only caught a single rafter or two, or maybe one floor joist, it is possible to effect a repair without undue hardship.

First, leave the rotted member in place. Clean it well with a wire brush (wearing gloves), and when it is thoroughly clean rub it well, with hard pressure, with handfuls of table salt. Rub the salt in hard, so it works back into the grain of the rotted area. (This is an old trick that dates back to the days of sailing ships, when rot, which is actually a form of rampant mildew, was a very real problem. They used to fill the spaces between the double hulls with rock salt.)

The salt will not reverse the rotting, indeed it does little but arrest the problem. After you have salted liberally, sandwich the rotted board with two new, good ones, nailed from both sides with 16d nails on 8-inch or 10-inch centers. The fix should hold for a long time.

Once again, the most important aspect of repairing rot is not the job you are working on at the moment, but preventing extended jobs that will be coming at you down the road. If you have rot problems now, you had best establish a good maintenance program to stop future rot. Check all the structural members, and if rot has started—or even if it hasn't—rub liberally with salt, so that it has been thoroughly worked back into the grain.

Remember when dealing with rot that panic is a great danger. Just because there's a touch of rot here and there doesn't mean the house is going to cave in. But it does mean that you will have to pay attention to steady maintenance.

chapter three
foundations

Foundations signify one of the paradoxes of home owning—you see it the least, and it often matters the most.

Of course as far as anything actually damaging the foundation of a house, the odds are relatively low. A hole is dug, cement or blocks are put down, the house is built on top, and that's the last you hear of it—or it should be.

Unfortunately many of the problems with foundations sometimes do not show up for years, and then they can be absolutely miserable.

Two of the most common will be examined, along with repair methods, but first a general word about difficulties with this type of work.

Everything to do with foundation work is heavy, dirty, back-breaking and foul. If any of those descriptions throw you off it might be best to bypass the work yourself, and call in a contractor. In either case, be careful of "quicky" fixes or shortcut jobs offered by supposedly professional foundation men. The quick cures to foundation problems rarely work.

Oh, a trouble that isn't a trouble is the famous hairline crack in the foundation. It scares many home buyers or owners, but actually does little damage. If it bothers you—and it's only a normal function of curing cement or settling loads—rub a bit of premixed cement in the crack with your thumb and forget it. Really. That is not what is meant by "foundation problems." Here are the two major ones.

Basement Water

By far the most common ailment with foundations is water seepage, especially in the spring, through the walls into the basement. It is caused by shoddy workmanship in initial construction of the home. The foundation wasn't waterproofed correctly, with plaster and/or *thick* tar, and adequate drainage (either with tube drain or drain tiles) was not provided.

Simplified drawing showing grading away from house to insure proper drainage.

It can cost you the use of half your house, cause the wood to rot faster and warp wildly because the humidity has increased so much, and generally be just a pain for as long as you own the home.

Sadly, if such damage has caught you, there is absolutely *no* shortcut or easy way to correct the problem. Repair is hard, miserable work and is usually quite expensive to boot.

If leakage is a problem, the only way to properly fix it is to dig down around the foundation of the house, down all the way to the bottom—the footing—and start from scratch.

Block Wall Foundation

First, using premix, it is necessary to plaster the wall if it is made of block. Mix the mud so it's fairly sticky and a shade runny, and apply it with broad strokes and a wide flat trowel, as in the illustration. Plaster it an inch thick, all the way from the footing up

15

There are no shortcuts to proper waterproofing. Go up in layers and do it right—one leak ruins it all.

to where the ground level starts, all around wherever the earth meets the foundation. It doesn't matter how it looks, just so it's thick and bonds well to the blocks. After some practice you will find it rather simple to plaster, although dirty.

Once the plaster coat is well set, which takes a day or two, coat it well with foundation tar. Again, really goop it on...thick. Then let the tar set for another day or two, and if the house is on a hill install a drain tube all around the footing with the two ends coming out the shallow or exposed end of footing. This allows the water to drain off before it gets into the house.

Concrete Foundation

If you have a concrete foundation, poured of cement, the process is exactly the same except that you do not plaster with cement. It is already effectively "plastered" when it is poured. But you still must tar thickly, and put in the drain tube if the house is on a grade so it will have adequate drainage.

It is miserable, messy, heavy work, but absolutely necessary if you want a complete repair. There is no easy way. Unfortunately the kind of repair where a plastic gunk is squirted down into the dirt along the wall is usually only partially effective, if that; it must *all* be done, all the way from digging down around the house to tarring, to be successful.

Because the repair is such a mess, reevaluate the problem before beginning the work.

First, check to be sure the water coming in is from seepage and not merely a small stream or something hitting the back of the house, in which case it could be diverted to stop the problem.

Second, can you live with the seepage? Seriously, if it isn't excessive, if it's merely a dampness, perhaps the problem isn't worth the work of repairing it. If a drain can handle it well, or an automatic sump-pump feeding into a drain, it might be best to avoid the whole mess of repairing and live with the problem.

The steps in repairing a damaged concrete slab. Top row (left to right): Preparing the surface by cleaning out all loose debris. Priming the surface. Next, a grout coating is placed. The grout of portland cement and water should have the consistency of thick paint. Bottom row (left to right): Placing and spreading mortar should follow immediately. Finishing the patch with a trowel. Repair completed. (Reproduced from Concrete Repair, Concrete Construction Publications Inc.)

Large Foundation Cracks

Less common, but still enough of a difficulty to be worthy of mention, are large cracks in foundations, whether block or poured cement. These cracks are more important for what they might mean than what they are.

Before considering repair, find the reason for the crack. If it is an inch or more at the top, it needs immediate repair. Curing cement rarely cracks very wide; if it is wide enough to see all the way through it probably means excessive settling in one corner because of inadequate footing surface.

Repair of the crack is simple. Mix up a very dry, almost crumbly, mixture of premixed cement and pack it, literally, into the crack. Dry cement cures stronger than wet, but more important it tends to slightly expand and fill the crack.

Really pound it in there, push it back in, and let it cure several days before painting or covering with siding.

The secondary effects are not as easy to stop. If the crack holds and stays full, fine. But if the crack is

Right and wrong method for patching a small shallow hole in a concrete wall or slab. (a) Wrong—This patch is too shallow. The featheredge will soon chip out, and this patch will not hold. (b) Right—The edges should be vertical. The patch is deep enough for a good body of mortar to be placed; this patch will stay.

caused by settling that is still occurring the crack will reappear in a few months. Watch it very closely and when it opens to a quarter inch or so repack it with a new dry-mixture of cement. If it just keeps expanding for years it could mean that the corner of the house is on a spring or some sort of slip rock (very rare), and it will be necessary to dig down and refoot the foundation; a massive repair and best done by a contractor.

Termites

Estimates show that termites cause close to $350 million of damage every year, although termite invasion can be recognized and caught at an early enough stage to prevent expensive repairs.

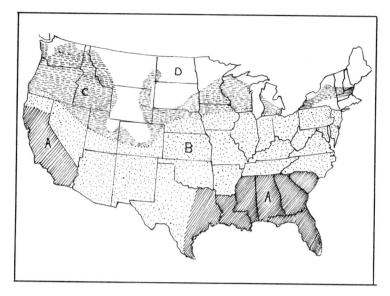

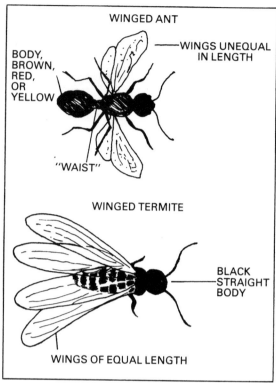

TERMITE SUSCEPTIBILITY BY GEOGRAPHIC AREA
A. Region I (including Hawaii): termite protection required.
B. Region II: termite protection generally required, although specific areas sometimes exempted.
C. Region III: termite protection usually not required, except specific local areas.
D. Region IV (including Alaska): termite protection not required.
SOURCE: U.S. Department of Housing and Urban Development (HUD) Minimum Property Standards. Washington, D.C.: Government Printing Office.

Winged ants are commonly mistaken for winged termites. Differences are noted in sketch.

The first areas to check for termite damage are earth-filled areas covered by concrete, such as steps, porches, or a landscape planter. From these areas termites can spread out to nearby wood. They then crawl upward through openings in slab or foundation walls; a crack as thin as a sheet of paper can admit termites. To cross exposed areas they build mud tunnels that are easily identified, usually spanning wood joists or sills. They also leave trails of sawdust. Look around the entire perimeter of your house for these tunnels or sawdust piles.

Inspection for termites is usually best carried out from below. Probe exposed wood parts with your screwdriver. If the point penetrates more than is normal, it may indicate termites. Where possible, remove any wood in contact with the ground, to deprive termites of access to your house.

Other protective measures include:
(1) adequate drainage;
(2) adequate ventilation;
(3) proper flashing;
(4) removal of all stumps, roots, or other wood debris;
(5) clearance between ground surfaces and lumber.

Corrective steps. Before resorting to an exterminator, try a commercial termite killer. Also replace outdoor wood with treated wood whenever possible. Add soil poison to porch slabs, planter boxes, and partially veneered sections.

Money-Saver Note

A money-saving thought on foundations. Many or most older homes are not adequately insulated, if at all.

This lack is most predominant where the house meets the foundation and it is not uncommon to find actual air-gaps between the sil plate and the foundation wall.

Go around and pack fiberglass insulation into the crack between the sill plate and the foundation; jam it in with a screwdriver or chisel and even hammer it a bit to make it tight.

Finally, look above the sill plate between the floor joists. If there isn't any insulation, cut squares and put them up between the joists as illustrated.

This does not count as an actual repair, but if you are down there anyway it can save some pretty good chunks on the heating bill.

chapter four

floors

Because there are so many different kinds of floors and floor coverings, there is no single common base for problem solving. Each floor is unique and has its own set of problems, and has to be fixed in its own way.

Floors are categorized and listed below, by type and problem.

Hardwood Floors

Becoming less predominant, good hardwood floors are now found only in expensive new homes and older dwellings. They are beautiful, and worth preserving, and for that reason a good maintenance

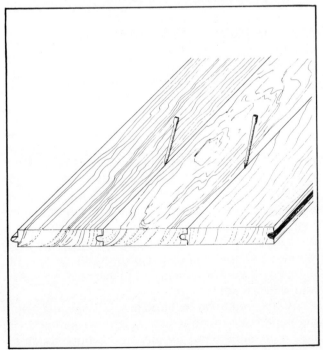

Just nail the finishing nails between the seams, setting them 1/8 inch and filling the tops with appropriately colored filler stick.

system is essential. Problems with hardwood floors are almost all due to aging.

Squeaking Floor

Generally caused by shrinkage and a slight pulling out of the nails, a squeaking hardwood floor is relatively easy to fix. First, try coating the floor with a thin, *good* floor oil, the kind that soaks in. Usually this will work down into the cracks and make the wood swell back toward its normal size, which in turn "tightens" the floor and stops the squeaking. If the squeak persists, try pounding the floor down, using a heavy hammer and buffer board, at the point of the squeak and out around in ever-increasing circles. If that does not work, and it probably will, find the floor joist nearest to the squeak and nail the two or three boards down that seem to be squeaking, as shown in the illustration. Be sure to nail at the seams, as it will spread the boards a bit and further jam them tighter. Use 8d finishing nails, and sink the heads in 1/8 inch. Then fill with precolored filler stick.

Lifting Boards

Over the decades hardwood flooring tends to lift as it shrinks and moves and the house settles. Standing back, with your face lowered, you can actually see that some of the boards are higher than others. Use a buffer board and heavy hammer, and with firm blows tap the floor back down where it seems to have risen. Mostly the boards will stay down, but for those places where they come back up, nail in the seams to joists with 8d finishing nails, sinking the nails 1/8 inch and filling with precolored filler stick.

Tipped or Canted Boards

Now and then, due to water damage or a faulty piece of wood, a floor board will appear to warp or

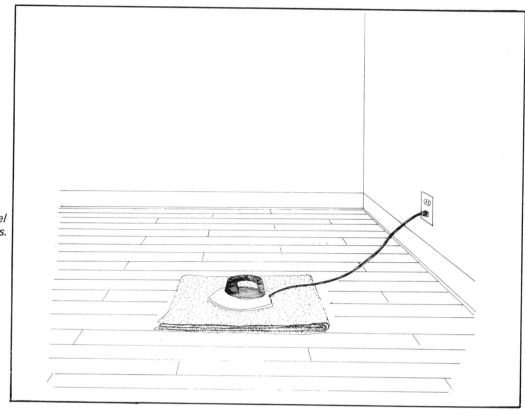

Use slightly damp towel and hot iron to lift dents.

turn one edge up—or more correctly, try to turn an edge up although the next board will hold it down. First try nailing on the seam, pulling the high side down into a floor joist. This will usually work; if you coat the nail with glue and use a 10d finishing nail for extra length, the board will stay down. If the board does not stay down, try taking a really damp towel and a hot iron and steam-ironing the warped part of the board for ten or fifteen minutes, really working the steam down into the crack. This usually softens the wood enough so that even the most stubborn board will stay down.

Finish Repair

There are many things which can go wrong with the finish on a hardwood floor—everything from puppy stains to sun-baking where light comes through the window and cooks the floor.

Basically, however, the repair method is the same whether it is a big area or a small one: the bad finish has to come off and the good finish has to go down and match whatever the surrounding area looks like.

If the floor finish has been destroyed over a large area, perhaps patchy over the whole floor space, the best method is to rent a huge buffer and do the whole floor with steel wool (fine) pads to lift the old finish and get down to raw wood. Sanding, using almost any grade sandpaper, is not to be recommended unless you have a good knowledge of the tools and materials. If you have never done it, it is a bear the first time and very difficult to do without messing up the floor.

But the steel wool pads do not chew down the way sandpaper does, and you'll find that once over will lift almost everything well. (Note: if you are doing corners where the buffer will not reach, do it by hand. You will find it much easier if you use a short piece of two-by-four covered with steel wool. The block allows you to press down and get more pressure.) With all the finish off it is a simple matter to refinish, using oils or gym-seal or any of several good floor finishing materials on the market. Just follow the instructions on the can for the floor color desired. The main thing is to be sure the old finish is thoroughly wooled off, completely gone, or the new one will not take evenly and will look spotty.

If the area to be repaired is small, say just a spot here or there, it is more difficult to make it match. But not impossible. First try any of the floor finish removers on the market. They are all about the same. Use conservatively, and allow everything to dry out well after each application. (For small patches of dis-

Machines are preferred for floor refinishing, and can often be rented. A large drum-type sanding machine with vacuum attachment is best for main floor area, while a power edger does sides as shown above.

Hand scraping is sometimes needed at edges and in corners even when using an edger-sander. Be careful not to gouge, and go over enough times to create a good surface, sanding with the grain.

coloration, where the floor is very dark, try a squirt or two of plain lighter fluid––it removes old finish and bleaches admirably for small areas.)

For pet stains, try a mixture of Seven-Up (yes, the soft drink) and lighter fluid. Just apply with a rag, let set for a few minutes, wipe off, let completely dry, and reapply as necessary to get the stain totally "lifted" and gone. Then refinish with oil, seal or wax as needed to match.

When spot refinishing hardwood floors be sure to "feather" the new finishing job into the surrounding old to make it fit in and match better. Work it out gently with a brush or rag to make it fit in.

Particle Board Underlayment

For economic reasons more and more homes are being finished with particle board floors. Tiles, sheets, or carpet are then put over the board. Repairing the overlayment will be covered shortly, but repairing the particle board and subfloor needs a quick mention.

Generally speaking, not much can happen to particle board. It is just there. The one thing, which does not happen often and yet can be devastating if it does, involves the house pipes: in certain areas of the country they can freeze and burst, and soak a particle board floor.

The particle board expands at a rate that is alarming. In a well-soaked floor it can rise up beneath the flooring and make "bubbles" as high as six or eight inches—large swellings all over the floor. And when it dries the floor does not come back down, either.

In this case the only repair is to remove the floor covering—carpet or tile or linoleum—and attack the board itself. After it has completely dried, use a rotary saw and a wide-cutting carbide blade and cut X patterns across the bubbles, as shown in the picture. These cuts will provide relief and, again, allow the under part of the cut to dry still further before further repair.

With everything dry, drill and pull the raised portions of the particle board down with wood screws, countersinking the screws so the flooring cover will not hit them.

This pulling-down method will work for the smaller bubbles. If there are truly large areas swollen up, the only repair is to cut out whole rectangles around the bubbles and throw them away and replace with appropriately cut new sections of board. Just set the blade on the rotary saw so that it only cuts the thickness of the particle board and be very careful that the saw doesn't "kick" out of the cut as

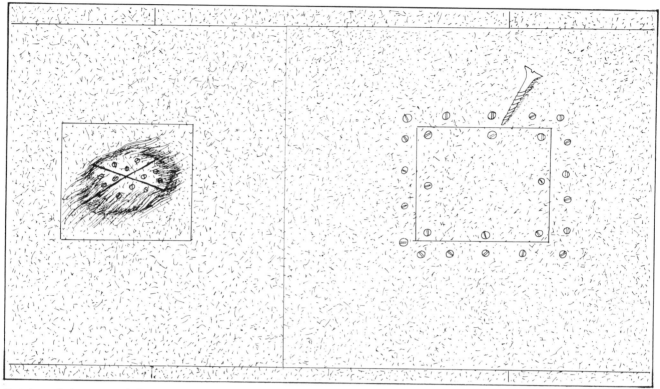

Cut the relief cuts carefully; two will usually be enough. Then pull down with screws.

you lower it in. (Cutting like this, lowering the saw into a cut, is very dangerous and shouldn't be done unless you are thoroughly familiar with power saws and know how to use them.)

When you cut out the repair spot in a whole rectangle, do not nail the new piece in. The nails will only work loose in a short time. The new piece of particle board has to be screwed down, with the screws going down well into the plywood subfloor and on eight inch centers. It also does not hurt to use a good construction adhesive underneath the new piece, and it is necessary to also sink screws in the pieces *around* the new one you're putting in—also on eight inch centers—lest the edges lift on the old pieces.

When done, and all the screws are well countersunk, cover with a good filler—or premixed drywall mud if you do not have filler—so that the repair job presents a smooth surface for flooring.

Carpet Repair

Replacing whole carpeted areas is not truly a repair and will not be covered here except to say that it is a tricky job, much trickier than it looks what with stretching and putting in the underfoam correctly.

But elemental repairs are possible without going through the difficulties of complete replacement, and they are listed below.

For tears made by moving furniture or whatever, do not completely rule out sewing. Just use correctly colored heavy thread (sail thread) and a curved upholstery or sail needle and sew up the cut with close, tight stitches. Tie it well when done and the repair will probably outlast the rest of the carpet.

If sewing does not seem adequate, get a heat-tape strip the right length from the nearest carpet or flooring store—this is a piece of fabric covered with strips of meltable glue. Put the strip under the cut with gum side up, running the length of the slit, and then cover it with a buffer cloth (old dishtowel) and iron the cut with the iron set on high. The iron melts the glue in a short time, it mixes with the fabric of the carpet and essentially welds the two edges together.

This same method can be used to fix whole sections of ruined or unwashably stained carpet. Cut out a square around the bad area, as small as possible but still get all the ruined material. Then cut a new piece the right size exactly to fit, and weld it in with heat-tape strips all around the new piece. If you both sew and tape, the repair is probably better than new carpet.

Put heat tape strip under carpet tear, gum side up, running the length of the damage. Cover with a buffer cloth and iron the cut with a very hot iron.

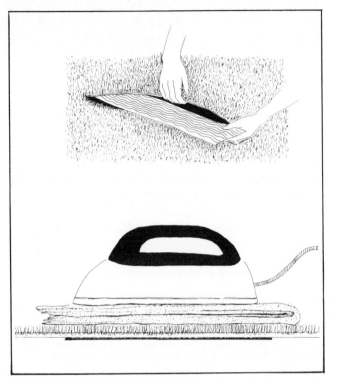

Stain removal is very tricky. There are so many different weaves and synthetic fabrics that using a bleach product can be murder. The best process for trying to remove stains is to use warm soap and water. If that does not work, use a strong detergent. And if that does not work, learn to live with the spot. *Solution for pet problem.* For those who have cats that have pulled up the little hooks of pile before you have had a chance to have the cats declawed: Try putting a tab of quick dry epoxy on the pulled-up end and tucking it back down into the mesh backing, being sure to poke the end through the mesh. When the glue sets it will look and hold as good as new.

Linoleum

The two things which most often go wrong with old linoleum floors are denting and tearing or cutting—mostly from moving appliances without lifting them.

In the case of dents, try a hot iron with a buffer towel. It does not always work, but sometimes it will get the job done and there is no other way to lift dents.

Broken tiles will come out easily to leverage with a screwdriver. Lay a new bed of adhesive with a puttyknife or other edge, and after waiting ten or fifteen minutes lay the new tile in.

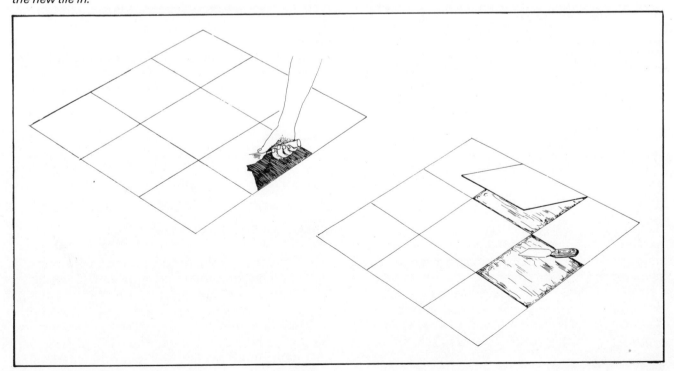

For cuts, gently lift the edges of the cut and work glue carefully back under both sides. Then put wax paper down on the cut and weight it down with a book or something as long as the cut.

When the glue has dried, use the correct colored felt tip marker or markers to recolor the glue in the crack to match the surrounding color and/or pattern. (Incidentally, this use of felt tip markers also works when you wish to recolor a place on the floor where a chair has scraped through the color.)

Composition (Asphalt or Vinyl Tile) Flooring

Composition tile flooring, usually glued down on concrete or on particle board, lends itself more readily to repair because it has been laid in individual squares and can be replaced easily.

To remove and replace a tile, which constitutes the basic repair for most tile floor problems, simply play a butane torch with a spreader head back and forth across the top of the tile from a height of five or six inches—so the heat is evenly distributed and does not get hot enough to ignite the tile.

The edges will curl, and once the whole tile is warm it will lift out easily. Be sure to wear gloves. With the old tile out, scrape-clean the open space, apply a thin layer of tile adhesive (being careful not to breathe the fumes), wait ten minutes and drop the new tile carefully in place. It will seat and stick immediately, but if you find the edges are not fastened down enough—sort of sticking up in the air—play the torch around the sides enough to soften the tile so it will lie down properly. (Just use the torch from the same distance, about five or six inches above the tile, keeping the flame moving constantly.)

Curled Tile

The only tile problem that does not require replacement of tile is when the tiles curl up or lift at the corners. This is usually due to the age of the floor. Repair is simple, but might involve considerable time if there are many tiles pulling themselves up. Use the butane torch and spreader head again, and after putting a small amount of glue under each corner and allowing the glue to set for ten minutes, soften the corners down into the glue by playing the torch back and forth from a distance of five to six inches.

Note. Do not let the torch come too close, as the tiles will easily melt and burn; it is better too slow than too fast.

Ceramic Tile Flooring

Becoming more popular as wood becomes more expensive, ceramic tiles create a durable and beautiful floor. Indeed, they have only two faults: (1) they sometimes crack, if they aren't set in right, and (2) they sometimes lift out of their grout.

Broken tile demands complete replacement, which is more difficult than dealing with composition tiles. The broken tile has to be "popped" out with a screwdriver, and then the opening has to be well brushed and clean. When you are certain the space is dry and clean, "fit" the new tile in place in the old grout. Do this dry, to make sure it is going to fit, and if there are any high spots where the grout pushes the new tile up or will not allow it to seat properly, carve these areas down using either a shop knife or coarse sandpaper. Make a close-fitting bed for the new tile or it will break like the old.

Finally, when the seat is just right and the tile does not wobble but sits firm, take it out and put down a 1/16 inch coating of construction adhesive. Set the tile in this immediately, press it firmly in place, and do not test it for two or three days.

For tiles which have lifted out of their grout but are still unharmed, the procedure is a simpler one. Just remove the tile, clean the blank space well—especially of dust, which has a way of filtering beneath tiles when they are loose—and apply a 1/16 inch layer of construction adhesive. (This is the kind you use like caulking, with a caulking gun.) Then settle the tile in place immediately, pressing down firmly.

Again, cleanliness is the most important item when working with ceramic tiles. Be certain the hole is clean and dust free, and then turn the tile over and clean the bottom with a damp rag, allowing it to dry well before putting it down.

Final note. Almost no luck was obtained trying to glue cracked tiles together, with any kind of glue, and then resetting them on a floor. Such an application will work with countertops, but the load on the floor is too much and the tiles almost invariably recrack.)

Sugarpine (Softwood) Floors

Almost nonexistent in new homes, the old softwood floors were made largely of sugarpine, a clear softwood. They are beautiful but terrible to maintain because they are so soft.

Repair methods are basically the same as with hardwood floors in all areas. You will find, however, that dents more readily "lift" out of the hardwood using a wet towel and iron than they do out of the softwood. Once the softer wood has been creased it does not bounce back so readily, if at all.

Some general thoughts to remember about soft floors:

• If you are sanding, be extremely cautious; the wood is just like butter to a power sander.
• Floor finishes will take more of everything to do the same job as for hardwood; the softwood soaks it up like a sponge.

Think rug: if you have a home with softwood floors—especially if you have children—the floors will be continuously dented without rugs to absorb some of the damage. Just dropping a toy metal tractor makes a dent that lasts forever, or until your next sanding.

Softwood shrinks at a much faster rate and to much greater degrees than does hardwood. Seams will actually open up. For this reason, consider a "wet" finish that keeps the wood from drying out over a long period—as with a good floor oil or *used* motor oil (which also makes a good finish for hardwood floors). Just wipe the finish on, let soak, wipe off the excess with an old towel.

Concrete Floors

Since most concrete floors are covered with another kind of flooring, and since they are virtually indestructible anyway, there is very little to be said about repairing them.

They do crack, however, with curing and age. This is no big problem and the cracks are normally little more than hairlines. If you wipe a dry mixture of premixed cement into the crack (assuming the crack is not covered with other kinds of flooring, in which case do nothing) and let it cure, it will fix things up for years.

Sometimes cement floors which are left unpainted will give off dust with heavy use. This is simply from the abrasive nature of walking, and can be easily fixed by applying any of several good sealers or paints found at the local paint store. But a word of caution: those sealers are extremely flammable and toxic to breathe; be sure that you pay attention to the safety rules on the can. Many houses have been lost to careless use of sealers and flammable adhesives. The fumes are like gunpowder, especially when confined in a basement.

Stone or Slate

Flagstone and Cobble Floors

Once limited to the patio, this category of flooring—either stone or brick cobble—is fast becoming a decorator's floor for indoors as well as out.

Stone or brick flooring is virtually repair-free once in place, assuming it has been installed correctly, but there are two ailments which deserve mention.

Cobble brick floors have a tendency to become "loose"; that is, the bricks start to wobble here and there when stepped on. This happens not because of improper seating, as might be expected, but because the buffer *between* the bricks has become compressed and allows them to move. For repair, mix a totally dry mixture of premixed masonry cement with pigment added to match the floor. Sprinkle this dry mixture around the loose bricks—still dry—and sweep and rub it down into the crack until it is packed in well and the brick no longer wiggles. Then use a flower sprayer or other kind of atomizer to put a fine mist of water around the crack and allow it to cure for two or three days, until it is well set. The floor will stay tight for years, and even then you only have to reapply the repair material.

Stone or flagstone flooring has a habit of cracking, especially the larger stones. There is no repair, as such, for cracked flagstones. You have to live with the crack. But once they break they also become loose and wobbly, and for this there is a repair. When the stone has become loose enough to pull out, take it straight up and out, being careful not to damage the grout around the stone. Then use construction adhesive—again, the kind that comes in a tube and you use with a caulking gun—and lay a ⅛-inch bed of glue in the empty space. Even this out with a straight stick or something else you can throw away, so the glue is a good, solid all-over bed for the wobbly or broken flagstone. Put the stone back in immediately, still being extremely cautious not to disturb the grout, and press it firmly but evenly into the glue. Put no further weight on the stone for at least two days, so the adhesive has time to cure and cradle the stone well.

Slate or Stone Floors

For broken out or cracked pieces of slate or stone flooring, relay the stone piece which has broken out in a ⅛-inch glue base (construction cement works well). Let dry for several days before walking on it.

Discolored slate or stone floors can be recolored with appropriately colored drawing ink—the kind that does not wash out. (There are literally hundreds of colors to use for matching—check your local art store.) Commercial stone quarry distributors also sell cleaning solutions that remove most stains.

When the color is all right, a treatment of a whole stone or slate floor with lemon oil will give a low gloss that looks rich and holds for days.

chapter five
interior walls and ceilings

Essentially, interior walls and ceilings can be broken down into two categories: either lath and plaster or drywall. The repair methods are somewhat different for the two forms of coating. For that reason this chapter will be broken down into three sections, with a final portion devoted to other kinds of walls.

Problems covered are those considered most common or most likely to occur, and the repair method suggested for each (often there are several different ways to fix the same problem) is the easiest and least expensive.

Lath and Plaster

Virtually no new homes are made of lath and plaster although it makes a strong wall and, many think, is prettier than drywall. But it costs so much in labor to put in, and lath and plaster craftsmen are becoming so rare, that people can't afford it.

Still, many older homes have it and repairing it properly can be a significant part of owning an old home. Some of the more typical problems with lath and plaster are listed below.

Small holes, dents or chips are the most common plaster problem. Usually caused by pulling out nails that held pictures, or moving furniture, the plaster tends to mar in a little crater and the smallest nail can make a pockmark an inch across. The repair is basic, quick and simple. Get a gallon can of premixed drywall mud—which is a good thing to keep on hand anyway—and use a putty knife or small drywall knife to fill the hole. Just one quick application, a single swipe, and let dry for a day before sanding with fine sandpaper and painting to match. (Take a paint sample from right next to the repaired spot; if you take a sample from too far away it might not match.)

Holes of considerable size can be patched in lath and plaster this same way; just one application of mud, let dry, sand, and paint to match.

When the damaged spots get big, two inches or more across, the work becomes more involved. The mud must be put on in two steps, the first a thick coat to fill the hole, and then a thin coat once the first coat has dried completely, as a finish. The undercoat will crack when it dries, but the second coat will fill the cracks. On very large patches—a foot across or more—it may take three coats, the final coat being very thin and sloppy (you can thin the drywall mud with plain water, just a bit at a time). Sand after the final coat, with fine paper, taking off the lumps or buildup, and paint to match the surrounding area. Be sure to "feather" the patch into the old plaster and sand it to further fit it.

Note. When sanding be safe and buy only the kind of drywall mud that *does not* have asbestos. Asbestos fibers, which they had in the old kind of mud, have been linked to certain forms of lung cancer, and it is dangerous to sand it without wearing a professional respirator mask.

There is no way to save plaster which has started to separate from the lath—usually in a ceiling after a bad leak. If it has already come loose, accept the loss and pull out what has come loose and is falling away; patch with drywall mud. This does not mean that you should jump to conclusions when you see a damp spot after a rain. First find and fix the leak, then let the plaster dry out completely, and it is probable that all you will have is a stain to paint over. Wet plaster most often dries out safe and sound. But if it gets really soaked it will visually separate from the lath, or it might even drop on your rug, and then you effect a repair.

On large patches, be sure to work the first coat of drywall mud well into any and all exposed lath, so that it "catches" well and holds. This is especially vital on ceiling repair, for obvious reasons. Also, on large patches, use a *wide* drywall knife—six inches or better. It is almost impossible to get a smooth patch over a large area with a small knife. (Sanding, by the

27

way, can take care of a wide range of mistakes. If it looks bad when you finish using the knife, don't worry; even the bumpiest ridges can be taken down with some sanding.)

Cracks

Hairline cracks are the most widely seen problem with lath and plaster, but are also easy to fix. Scrape the crack with a paint scraper, down the long way, and not too heavy; the idea is to remove some of the paint and loose plaster to get a good bond with the patch. Then just use a narrow drywall knife to run a thin layer of mud down the length of the crack, forcing it into the crack with steady pressure. Wipe off excess and allow to dry thoroughly overnight. Then sand with a light touch and paint to match. The crack will absolutely disappear.

A final note on lath and plaster: Most plastered walls and ceilings are smooth, and repairs should match. But now and then the homeowner will run across a textured wall or ceiling, and he/she obviously cannot use a smooth repair. The way to get a texture to match the old is to mix up a small amount of drywall mud into a gloppy sort of thick paint; just keep adding water until the consistency reaches thin fudge. Then wet a towel, or a mop, or a piece of scrap carpet, and pat some of the mixture onto the patch. Try different items, including your hand or the side of your fist, until you find something that will match the existing texture fairly closely. It does not have to be exact, but just close, and when it looks about right let it dry for a couple of days before painting to match.

Drywall Walls and Ceilings

In most respects, repairing drywall is the same as repairing lath and plaster, except that it is easier.

Small holes, dents, gouges from moving furniture or children playing can be fixed with a dab of premixed drywall mud. They also make a powdered form of drywall cement: spackling paste, joint cement, joint compound, joint mud, taping mud, sheetrock mud, rock mud, wallboard mud; it's all the same. This powdered mud is fine and will do the job nicely, but it is a struggle to mix it without lumps and to get the right texture for patching. The premixed comes just right and you can reseal the can for storage. As with lathe and plaster, just give the small hole or crack or dent or gouge a quick swipe with the mud on a small knife, let dry, sand, and paint to match.

You must paint drywall mud, by the way. Even if

it matches the white of the rest of your wall when dry, if you do not paint it the material will never seize properly and a little will rub off every time you touch it. But as with plaster repair, be certain the patch is totally dry before applying paint. Wait overnight or longer.

Larger holes in drywall can be fixed in several ways, all simple. The easiest is to cut a square or rectangle around the hole, as small a square or rectangle as you can to still cover the complete hole. Then you cut a piece of drywall (with a shop knife or sabersaw) so that it will just snugly fill the hole. With everything clean of dirt and dust on both the hole and the cut patch, put wet drywall mud around the side of the opening and around the patch and gently put the patch in place using the drywall mud as glue to hold it in. With extreme care, wipe off the excess mud and allow to dry well—overnight—before the next step.

When totally dry, sand the drywall lightly and "tape" the seams all around. Taping drywall is tricky but easy to learn. You first apply a thin coat of drywall mud to the seam, about 3 inches wide, and put a precut piece of drywall paper tape on the seam. Do this for all four sides, as shown in the illustration, and again let dry for a few hours. When reasonably dry, apply another layer of mud over the tape—still thin, still about 3 inches wide—and feather this out into the surrounding wall. Let dry well, sand lightly, paint to match the wall. (A note about being afraid of all this: in the end all you've really lost is some time. It is not hard to do, and if you take your time the job will wind up looking as polished and well done as that done by any professional. But even if all your work is

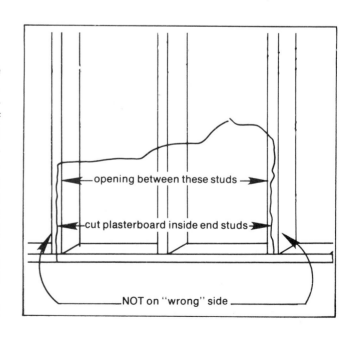

opening between these studs

cut plasterboard inside end studs

NOT on "wrong" side

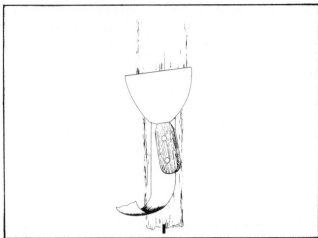

Taping drywall.

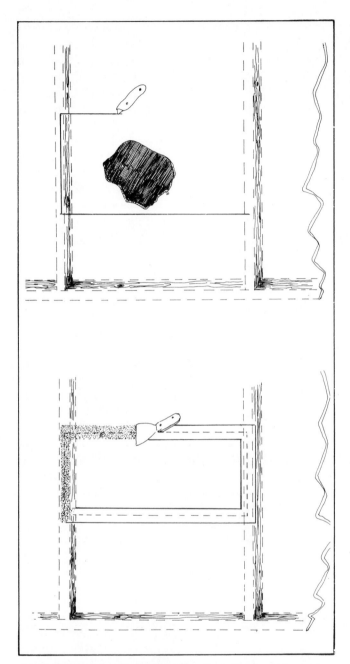

Cut out the old with shopknife, nail and tape and mud in the new. Don't worry that it doesn't look good right away; sanding will shape it up fast enough.

for nothing, you can still call the contractor. No large amount of money has been spent, no damage has been added; all you have lost is a little time.)

For truly large holes in drywall—broken pipes bringing ceilings down like wet sponges—for massive damage the repair is almost easier.

Just cut the drywall out between studs or rafters, going from the middle of one stud to the next (the stud or rafter will be easy to find in a hole so big) and

cut a new piece to fill the hole. Nail this new piece in place using drywall nails on 4 inch centers, so the repair section spans the whole distance between studs or rafters, as shown in the sketch.

Then tape the joint, taking your time and using a wide knife, sanding evenly between coats of mud if necessary to get a good looking seam. When it is done, and dry, paint to match.

Two points to remember about working with drywall mud, especially overhead. It stings in your eyes, so you might want to wear goggles or safety glasses when you work. And when you sand drywall mud it gives off a fine, irritating sneezy dust. If you have bronchial problems, use a nose-and-mouth cover.

Finally, we look at the most common and utterly needless drywall repair job, which is sadly becoming more and more common: the lifting seam, or tape coming loose on a fairly new home. The problem is that the drywaller did not get enough mud under the tape during the original taping and the adhesive qualities did not take—another way of saying shoddy workmanship. The repair involves taking a wide drywall knife—six inches—and putting new drywall mud in the seam. Just spread a layer of mud right over the lifted tape and paint, old wall and all—don't worry, the new mud will take. When it is dry, sand a bit and add another layer if necessary to "feather" it out into the wall for an even surface, and when that is all dry and sanded, paint to match.

For textures, as with lath and plaster, mix up a thick drywall mud, so it is like paint, and start experimenting with different objects to get a good matching texture. Try sponges, sacking, whatever it takes to look right, but a small helpful hint: most drywallers like to texture with a very heavy-nap paint roller, because it covers fast and thick. If the texture on your wall looks very even, you might try a heavy-nap roller. It will probably match out just right.

Oh, perhaps it goes without saying, but be certain to use a drop cloth when doing overhead work. Wet drywall mud does not come out of carpet easily.

Other considerations on drywall: on major problems such as burst pipes in ceilings or wind damage, do not try to save the drywall. Even with skyrocketing prices on building materials it is cheaper to buy new drywall. Just rip out the whole damaged sheet, pull the nails and apply a new sheet, and tape to fit in. Also, drywall walls painted with latex based paints seem to attract smudges and stains at an appalling rate. One kid, with a peanut butter and jelly sandwich, can ruin what seems like a thousand square feet of wall in ten minutes. Many paints are washable, or so they say, but by far the quickest fix on smudged up walls is to repaint. Repair for this particular problem will be found in the paint and finish chapter.

Don't underestimate the dirtiness of working drywall: most work with sheets of drywall is done with a sharp shopknife; just cut and break on the line. But now and then it is necessary to cut with a handsaw or sabersaw (to cut a piece out of the wall), or with a hand drywall saw (which looks like a keyhole saw). No matter what the saw, the sawdust is unbelievable. It goes everywhere, gets into everything. But if you have a friend hold up the wide open end of a running vacumn cleaner hose right along the cut you are making, you will find that the dust almost magically disappears.

Other Wall Coverings

Other wall coverings lend themselves pretty much to a common sense approach.

Wood

Paneling can be patched with appropriately colored wood filler compound. If you have a lot of panelling it wouldn't hurt to keep a couple tubes around. They are inexpensive and easy to store. Make sure to get the right color—check it by application—and then store in a cool dry place. The filler really works well for nail holes when you pull out a picture, or to fill in dents or tears. As far as the general finish goes, there are many good finishing agents for wood panelling. They all leave a shine and furnish adequate protection, but they tend to cost. For the money it is hard to beat plain old fashioned wood oil—even some of the lemon type—which does not cost as much as the spray cans and gets the job done as well.

Raw wood walls. Barn wood is the classic example; it can be repaired by replacement, just as with external siding (see the chapter on siding repair). Be careful when hammering, as the wood is soft and interior hammer dents show when the light changes. If you do make a dent, it can be lifted out with a damp towel and hot iron—just steam it up, which works well in all dented wood problems. If pieces of the wood wall have been broken out, do not jump to an expensive replacement conclusion. Before tearing the rest of the board out, consider gluing the piece back in. Use a strong, clear-drying glue and follow directions on the tube carefully. Do not rush anything. If a whole long piece of wood has split off, it would not hurt to "peg" the repaired section. After the glue has set and dried thoroughly drill a couple of small holes up through the split piece into the larger one (just use a drill bit the size of wooden matches) then push some wooden matches with ends soaked in glue up into the hole (see sketch) and when the glue is dry cut them off with a razor blade or utility knife. Stain the little ends of the matches by dabbing a bit of color on them (felt tip pen, wood stain, whatever you have that looks right) to match them in. This pegging is not truly necessary, but gives the repair extra strength and will help if the siding is low enough to get bumped by furniture.

Wallpaper Repair

Wallpaper dropped out of vogue for a while but is coming back as a covering. It is a virtually repairless surface. If it goes bad, start from scratch because it is patterned and hard to match up. One common problem is "lifting," when the paper comes up or bubbles. If it lifts on a seam, simply apply a dab of wallpaper wheat paste and press it back down. If the bubble is in the middle of a sheet, slice with a razor blade, use a toothpick to gently work paste back under into the bubble and then press down. Do not use mucilage glue or airplane cement; you can't wipe it off. Flour and water paste or commercial wheat paste can be taken off the surface with a damp rag once the repair is finished.

Wallpaper—From Scratch

Many people pay out their money so a contractor or handyman can strip off or put up wallpaper

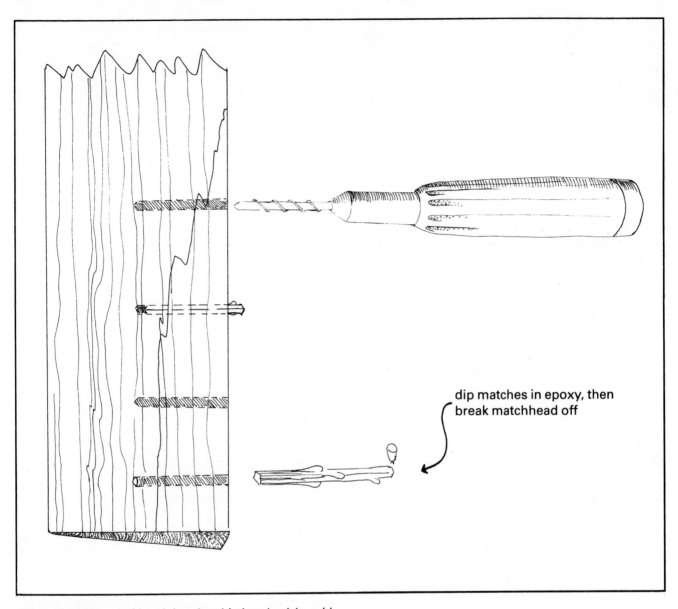

dip matches in epoxy, then
break matchhead off

*After repairing wood by gluing the old piece back in, add
extra strength with "pegging": all you need are some
matches, a screwdriver, some epoxy, a color marker, and
a utility knife or razor blade.*

although this is one job that offers savings to the homeowner without potential hazard or unprofessional-looking results.

Removing Old Wallpaper. Remove old wallpaper unless it adheres firmly to the surface, especially where the seams join and at the edges in the ceiling —or at any protruding surface such as a window sill or molding.

You can tell whether or not the covering adheres firmly by cutting out two square feet of the wallpaper you plan to use and applying paste to half of it. Apply the whole square, which means that one half will hang loose; let stand overnight. Then tear off the unpasted section, which will pull up pasted paper as well. If the old wallpaper beneath the newly pasted part comes off too, then you know the old wallpaper has to be removed.

Another tip: if there is a plastic coating on the old wallpaper, use an alkyd primer-sealer before applying the new wallpaper. Use a similar coating over old wallpapers that have become dry and chalky.

Depending upon the tenacity of the old wallpaper, you may have to try several methods of removal. The first and easiest approach is to saturate the wallpaper with hot water and then scrape it off. If this does not work, try a commercial wallpaper remover to heighten water penetration and speed the job. Or rent a wallpaper steamer for large scale removal. But never use a steamer near fine furniture, cabinets, or floors. Experienced contractors prefer to use them only in empty rooms, with windows open.

If you are removing foil covering or one overcoated with water-resistant material, use sandpaper or an abrasive of some type to bite shallowly into the surface. This will enable you to reach the water-absorbant material. Then saturate, using a light mist from a hand sprayer or sponge.

Once the wallpaper has been removed, be sure to work off all adhesive; hot water applied with a slightly abrasive pad will usually do it. Be careful not to gouge the walls. Then spackle to smooth out any depressions. Also tape and spackle joints between preformed wall components such as plywood or drywall, because joints are often improperly joined.

After pasting smoothly, fold paste to paste so edge ends up just short of center of strip, pattern up. Fold other edge to just beyond the edge of other fold, which should have a few inches without adhesive. Do not crease folds.

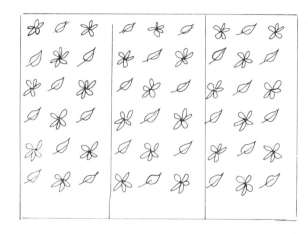

In a drop-match pattern, once you line up the marks, you will find that the first strip has the full pattern at the top. The number two strip will have a half-pattern at the top; the number three strip will also have the full pattern at the top. These three strips illustrate a drop match pattern. Note that every other strip is the same at the top.

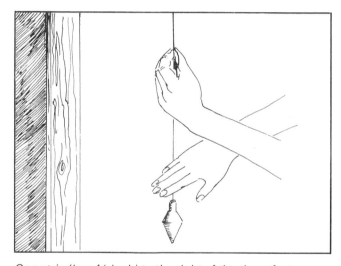

One strip (less ½ inch) to the right of the door, fasten plumb line from ceiling. Chalk the string and, holding it near the bottom, snap a line onto the wall. Measure ceiling height. Allow 3 inches extra top, 3 inches at bottom.

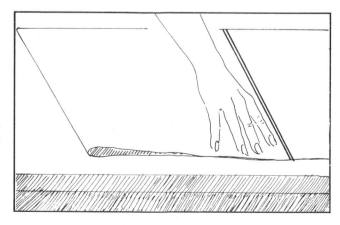

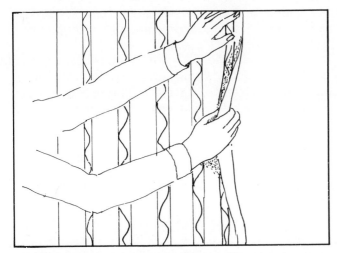

Unfold top part of strip only. Position near ceiling, leaving 3 inches to trim off later. Line up the right edge of the strip with the plumb line.

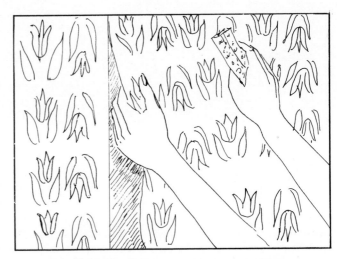

Hang succeeding strips. Carefully match pattern at left edge of new strip with previous strip. Butt edges, sponge, and roll edges.

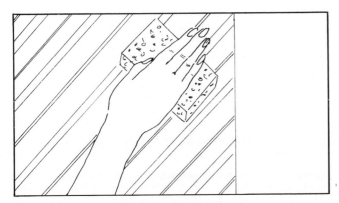

Smooth strip, working from center to edges. Unfold bottom, align with plumb line, smooth out entrapped bubbles with sponge. Small bubbles disappear with drying.

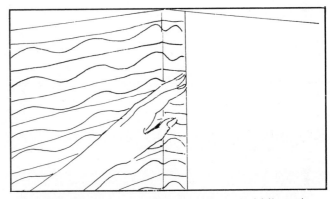

At corner: Measure edge-to-corner at top, middle and baseboard. Take widest measure; add ½ inch. Cut vertical strip this width. Apply, overlap corner ½ inch. Measure next strip. Add ½ inch. Drop plumb this distance from corner. Follow plumb; apply, match pattern and lap at corner.

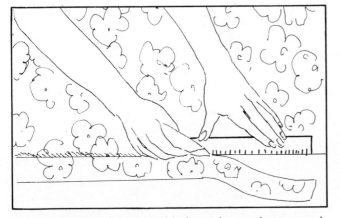

Use ruler with knife or razor blade to trim top, bottom and around door frame. Wipe off paste with wet sponge. Smooth entire strip. Roll down edges with a seam roller. Don't use roller on flock wall coverings. Tap seams with sponge to avoid matting flock pile.

Windows: Measure ceiling to frame. Add 1 inch. Cut vertical strip, apply so it extends over top of frame 1 inch. Trim around frame. Match pattern; use short lengths above, below frame.

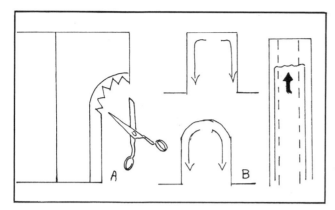

Application at arches: (a) to prevent fraying at edges make small cuts ½ inch apart so wallpaper will wrap on the inside of the arch without wrinkling; (b) if doing the top section of the arch, cut your strip so it is long enough to start hanging from the inside top in the middle, then continue down each side. The mismatch will not be seen underneath. Remember to (c) leave ½ inch overlap on each edge of the wallpaper used underneath, ¼ inch of which goes under the covering used on the outside. Leave ¼ inch space between edge of arch and wallpaper covering placed as overlap, to prevent fraying or peeling at overlapping edge.

Once the spackle has dried use a primer-sealer so the porous components won't suck in the adhesive, which would make it hard to remove the wallpaper the next time around.

If walls are old and appear porous, or you have old wallpaper with a fine dust or powder you just can't completely remove, treat the area with a glue size or emulsion bonding agent. There are several types on the market: cold water natural powder and the jellized size risk mildew under materials that do not breathe, such as vinyl, foil, or Mylar. For these products use a synthetic size.

Another possible answer to minor irregularities in surface and adhesive control, particularly for sensitive materials such as silk and textiles, is paper lining. The acid-free type is more expensive but avoids possible chemical damage. Be sure to leave ⅛ inch gap at ceiling, baseboard, window, and door casings so the wallpaper can bond to the wall; this will prevent lifting.

Cutting Steps. Roll wallpaper out on paste table. Trim off selvages using carefully placed straightedge. Locate the point at which you want the pattern to begin on the wall; this is where the paper will meet the ceiling edge. You will be looking for the point at which a full pattern begins. (Note: Be sure the top of the material is to your left.) From the point selected, measure the height of the wall, and add 2 to 3 inches extra from the top point of the pattern, and the same at the bottom. Use a straightedge at right angles and cut the strip off with a razor blade.

If the wallpaper has a drop-match pattern (see sketch) you will have to move down to catch a full pattern, which leaves a great deal more than 3 inches of excess. Cut off all but 3 inches at top and bottom to prevent extra wallpaper from interfering with hanging.

With a quarter-drop pattern (even more complicated than a drop-match) use four rolls; number each roll, one through four, for each step in the pattern. After marking numbers, match join-points so the second, third, and fourth strips in a sequence move along the pattern as you go to the succeeding strips. *Note:* If stiffness makes it difficult to trim selvages, leave them on the first and second strips and match up the pattern while hanging them. This means one selvage goes beneath the other, and top selvage flaps over the edge of the pasted-down wallpaper. Then cut through both selvages to end up with a double-cut seam. Lift up the wallpaper that covers the cut-off selvage which ended up underneath; remove strip of cut selvage; re-adhere edge of strip. Repeat for remaining strips.

Pasting Tips. Lay strips face down on a table, making sure you have a smooth surface. Again, place the top of the wallpaper to your left. Load a seven-inch paint roller with a ⅜ inch nap with just enough paste so it doesn't drip. Draw it down the middle of the strip, starting about 2 or 3 inches from the top end so you can leave unpasted the area to be trimmed off. Continue halfway down the strip. Work the paste on this strip toward both edges. This gives a smooth coat and avoids smears. The roller also contributes to a more even coat. Repeat procedure for the bottom half of the strip.

The accompanying photos and illustrations offer basic steps in matching, cutting, and hanging.

Tile

Tile walls are commonly used in bathrooms but are becoming prevalent in kitchens as well; they have two problems. Either the adhesive comes loose or the tiles crack. If the adhesive is the culprit, simply buy some tile adhesive and reglue the loose piece. Directions for the process are on the glue can. If one is loose, however, it is possible that there are others and you should check this by using your fingers to gently "rock" each tile. If the glue is coming loose the tile will move and it is a simple matter to pull the tiles out and recement. For cracked tiles the obvious solution is to pull out the broken tile and glue a new one in, and nine times out of ten this is the proper procedure. Still, sometimes a replacement tile is not available or cannot be found, and it becomes necessary to reuse the old tile. Take out the cracked pieces and glue them together with a *good* glue (quick drying epoxy-base glue is nothing short of incredible for this application). Let the glue dry well, for a full day, so that it is properly hard, then reglue the tile in place on the wall with a thick base of tile adhesive to give it a cushion and prevent a recurrence of the crack.

A last thought on wall coverings. There are several companies that have recently brought out vinyl plastic wall panels. Generally speaking, they are repaired using common sense, as is anything. Gouges or dents will not iron out, however, and must be filled with appropriately colored filler; a wood filler will work. Also, the finishes will "melt" if hit with something hot—poker, cigarette end, etc.—and there is no repair except replacement of the whole sheet (that is, if a filler doesn't work). You cannot remelt the finish and reform it. If, however, you cannot get a new piece of vinyl sheeting, you might try cutting the melted piece out and refilling with fiberglass putty. When it is hard and set—well set—paint to match with plastic model cement, either gloss or matt as the situation dictates.

The final type of plastic described here is not typically a wall covering, but might be. Countertops are covered with this hard-surfaced sheathing and it sometimes runs up the wall. Generally the only problem is that the glue allows it to come away from the undersurface; it is a simple matter to reglue it with cement from the local lumberyard. Chips, which happen now and then, virtually cannot be fixed and must be lived with. But now and then, caused by putting a too-hot pot down, the surface will get a wrinkle or dimple. Repair is to heat an iron and hold it a half inch or so over the dimpled area. Too close and you will burn it, too far and the fix won't take. As the heat softens the surface it will go back to its previous shape and texture—then, right then, remove the iron, and allow the surface to cool slowly at room temperature.

chapter six

windows, screens, & drapes

There was a time, and not too long ago, when properly repairing windows was one of the things few people could do easily. Homeowners had to mix their own putty, which is tricky at best and disastrous at the worst, and cut their own glass. . . .most people gave it up and just called the glazer. And rightly—for the uninitiated, just cutting a pane of glass the right size is almost impossible.

But things have changed drastically. Premixed, plastic glazing compound—putty—comes in small, inexpensive cans. Glass stores have come into being—usually paint and glass stores—and are so numerous you can get precut glass panes at little extra cost.

The main thing to remember is to wear gloves, avoid cutting, and take your time. Below are listed the more common windows and their replacement procedures.

Windows

Standard Panes, Wooden Window

The classic paned window, which has been around for centuries, is probably still the easiest to repair.

If at all possible, replacement glass for broken window panes should be tempered to prevent future breakage. This safety precaution is particularly important for sliding doorwalls and for storm windows.

When you have a broken pane of glass, the first step is to break out the rest of the broken glass; push it out with a stick and steady gentle pressure—wearing gloves. When all the glass has been broken out, clean out any and all remaining old putty and use a dull knife or chisel to scrape out the wooden area (the little ledge) where the glass fits in—it is called a rabbet.

With the rabbet now clean measure the size of the replacement window needed and take off just a bit, maybe a sixteenth of an inch. Then get a piece of glass cut the correct and slightly smaller size at the nearest lumberyard or glass store. While you are there get a small can of window glazing compound and a putty knife and some glazing points. About these points: for the unprofessional it is easier to use the kind that are shaped like folded little arrows rather than the flat ones.

Back at the rabbet, put the window in and use the putty knife to jam the glazing points in place as per instructions on the glazing point box, and the illustration below.

Push the glazing points in straight, with even pressure, and don't push against the glass too hard.

Put two glazing points on each side of the glass, which should be the same thickness as the glass that was broken, and that will hold it.

Glazing, the actual putting in of the putty, tends to be easy if you relax and aren't too fussy.

First roll the putty between your hands to make a long tube about ⅜ inch thick. Press this tube gently into the corner of the window glass, where it meets the rabbet, so the tube goes all the way around the pane.

Then take the putty knife, and holding it at an angle use it to compress the putty down into the joint as shown in the illustration.

Do not "cut" the putty or shave it off, but mash it as you pull the knife along the tube of putty. The excess putty will ooze out the sides; the part that gets mashed down will form a nicely beveled edge.

It is much easier than you first think and after a bit of practice you will find it goes very smoothly.

Unless it says otherwise on the can, and there are several new substances on the market that might note it on the instructions, do not paint until the glazing compound has had a few days to set in and cure.

After a bit of practice you'll find the excess putty just seems to roll down away from you.

Large Wooden Windows With Nailed Stops

Many homes built lately have simple wooden windows with large sections of glass held in by nailed strips of wood known as stops instead of using glazing points and putty.

Repair is easy. First remove all the broken glass, wearing gloves and safety goggles because glass flies all over when it snaps and the little invisible pieces can damage your eye. Clean out all the glass and take it away and put it in the trash before going any further. Do not leave the broken glass lying around, because that is invariably where your knee will come down if you fall.

With all the glass gone it is time to remove the outside stops—the wooden "lips" that hold the window in place.

This can be done one of two ways. You may carefully take a wide wood chisel and work the stop loose by prying, but an excessive care must be taken to avoid denting the wood. Or you can use a very thin, long nail punch to drive the finishing nails on through to the other side of the stop.

Either method demands great care and the worst thing you can do is hurry. Also, while taking out the stops, number them and make certain they go back in *exactly* the order they came out. Houses settle with age and window frames may move a bit; if you do not put them back the way they came out they probably will not fit.

With the stops out use a chisel to clean the dried caulking and/or gunk out of the place where the window will set. Then measure the opening and get a piece of glass cut to fit, but slightly smaller to avoid problems—again, just a sixteenth of an inch or so.

While you are at the hardware or glass place get a small caulking gun and a tube of window caulking compound. It won't hurt to have the gun around for other uses, and it is not too expensive.

While at the glass store tell the clerk the type of window you are putting in and ask what size glass you should be using—and whether or not it has to be crystal or plate. None of it is critical, but with expert advice available free you might as well use it.

Back at the window lay a bead of caulking all around the window opening, all the way into the corner where the stop meets the sill. This you can allow to set a bit, just a few minutes, so it will not be runny and sticky, and then put the window in place. Wear gloves and work it back into position slowly a little at a time all around the glass. Window glass will bend a little, especially the bigger pieces, but the instant it warps too much it shatters. So go a little at a time, all around. Work it back into the caulking until it is well stuck and then put the stops in.

Insert the top one first, nail with 6d galvanized finishing nails; nail with all caution. It helps to put a piece of cardboard or fiberboard against the glass to protect it from the hammer, and to nail in the same holes from which the nails came out.

Follow the edge of the glass with the stops and do not put undue strain by pushing the stops back in too hard against the glass. The whole window frame might be slightly askew and you can't fix it by "bending" the glass.

Wooden Window With Routed Sash Rails and Stiles

Some windows have the glass put in at the factory, with in carved out and routed grooves. When such windows break the repair is so difficult that perhaps only the experienced should try it.

It is necessary to literally hack out the glass from the front of the rails and stiles with a chisel or knife, pick the glass out, sand all the rails and stiles so they look good (and they almost never will), individually cut the new panes to fit this ragged hole, and putty the glass in.

What is so strange is that these windows cost a lot of money. They should be free.

Many, most new homes have aluminum window systems for economic reasons and ease of installation.

Happily, they are also the easiest to repair if they have been installed correctly. Repair is simply a matter of removing the broken glass, taking out the screws that hold the frame together and putting in the appropriately cut (slightly smaller) repair piece of glass.

You will find a plastic piece of insulation barrier, sort of a permanent caulking strip; make sure this goes around the new glass just as it went around the old piece. Then screw the frame back together.

Note: sometimes you will find the builder put the frame in wrong and nailed down those portions of the frame which are supposed to be loose and unscrewable. If this is the case, the nails must be carefully worked up and out with a screwdriver or catspaw before you can effect a regular repair.

Added thought: it perhaps goes without saying to be sure to remove the screen. It lifts up and out with those little tabs—before you start repairing the window.

Replacing Wooden Windows with Aluminum

The main thing about replacing wood windows with aluminum is not to take too much out. Remove all the weatherstrips with a screwdriver; take out the old wooden window; clean the opening—but leave the sill and stops in place. Now the window is preframed and you simply buy aluminum windows which will nail into the framed opening snugly (they make all sizes).

Just remember to caulk under the edges with colored caulking when nailing in the new window.

Installing Prefabricated Wooden Windows in Old Openings

Again, remove only what is necessary to get the opening down to the size of the new window assembly—and never remove any structural frame members. Take out the old weatherstrips and windows, then clean the sills and sides and fit the new window into the opening, nailing in with 10d finishing nails. Fill holes, and paint.

Picture and/or Plate Windows

Repair methods are the same for large windows as they are for small. The broken glass goes out, then you clean, caulk, and put the new glass in.

But for large picture windows or store plates there are some added cautions to make the job safer and easier.

Always wear gloves, and get somebody to help you when it is time to put the new window in. It is extremely difficult to do it alone.

Watch warpage. Large pieces of glass are especially prone to twisting and breakage. Do not force anything, ever. It will all come apart on you. When you get the new piece of glass cut, give yourself a good ⅛ inch of play all around, plenty of room, and caulk liberally when you put the new piece in.

Finally, evaluate the kind of window you are putting in and how much money you want to spend.

Plate is very flat, and quite expensive, but virtually cancels out the "wobbly" effect which shows up so much on large windows. Crystal is much less expensive, and every bit as good for letting light in. However, it will have a wobble here and there, and if the picture window you are putting in or repairing is for unobstructed viewing, you might want to go to plate.

Installation or repair methods are the same for either one.

when and how to replace a faulty window

More than likely even if your home is considered old and you've repaired and repainted and refinished many parts of it, you haven't replaced the windows. If your windows are in poor condition, they can be weatherstripped and you can add storms, but also consider replacing the units altogether.

How can you tell when it's time to replace windows? Be on the lookout if your windows just don't seem to be doing what they're supposed to. Does the outside view seem blurry? Do you always have to prop your window open because it won't stay that way by itself? Do you constantly have to caulk and weather strip your windows because of the drafts? With enough "yes" answers to those questions, you may have reached the point of no return where your time and money on repairs simply aren't worth the investment.

Until a few years ago this was a very costly undertaking, but many window manufacturers today are offering custom-fit windows which require no structural alteration. By following the instructions here, you should be able to do the job efficiently.

Then remove sash.

Remove window trim to free sash.

Using screwdriver for leverage, remove wooden channels and all other obstructions.

Assemble new unit according to manufacturers instructions. The next three photos show how one unit goes together.

When unit is assembled, make sure that it fits squarely into the space. If space is not square use wooden shims to make window fit. Do not bend frame to make it fit space!

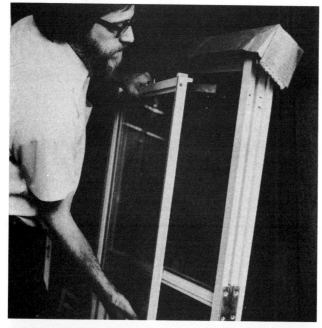

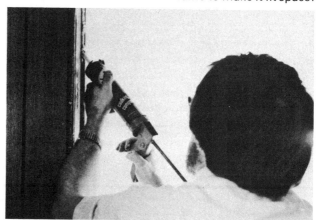

Remove window and apply generous amount of caulking before installation.

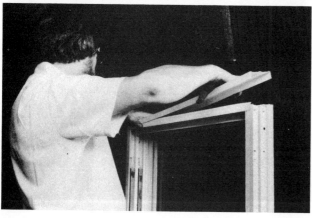

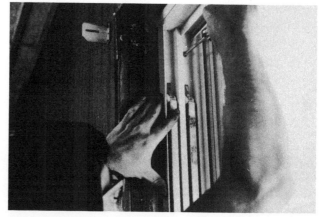

Set window into opening and tighten down screw at one corner. Then square and plumb unit for final adjustment.

Fasten remaining sections of window in place as shown in next two photos. As you tighten down the screws, make sure you do not bend the unit to meet the wall. If wall is warped, use a shim behind window to maintain square.

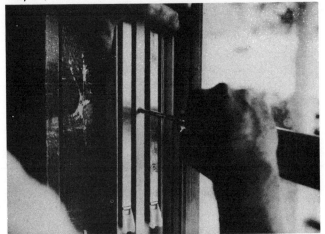

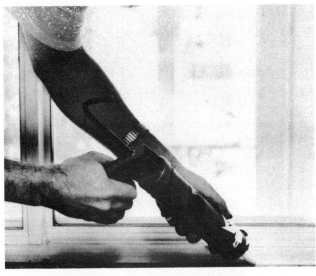

Caulk between new window and inside wall.

Install sashes according to manufacturer's instructions.

Put up new molding unit around window. (Photos courtesy of Season-all Industries, Inc.).

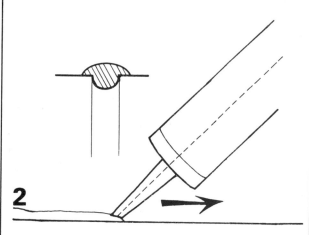

1

Before applying caulking compound, clean area around window of paint build-up, dirt, or deteriorated caulk with solvent and putty knife or large screwdriver.

2

Drawing a good bead of caulk will take a little practice. First attempts may be a bit messy. Make sure the bead overlaps both sides for a tight seal.

3

A wide bead may be necessary to make sure caulk adheres to both sides.

caulking windows

How To Weatherstrip Windows

To weatherstrip your windows and doors you'll need a hammer, nails, screwdriver, tin snips and tape measure. It usually takes less than one-half hour per window. You have a choice of installing at least three different types of weather stripping. There is no sense in paying a contractor to do this type of work.

Metal strip

This strip is installed into the channel of the window or door so that it is virtually invisible. Because this weather stripping is metal, it is very durable. It doesn't need much maintenance but is somewhat difficult to install. Costs about $2 per window.

Rolled vinyl

It is available with or without metal backing; is durable, easy to install, but visible. Cost under $2 per window.

Foam rubber with adhesive backing

The least expensive, it is extremely easy to install but is also the least durable. It breaks down quickly, particularly where friction occurs, so you may be back weather stripping next autumn. Cost is pennies per foot.

Thin spring metal

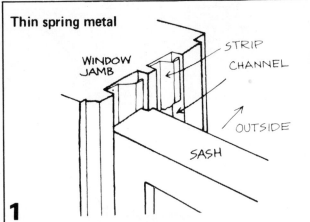

1

Install by moving sash to the open position and sliding strip in between the sash and the channel. Tack in place into the casing. Do not cover the pulleys in the upper channels.

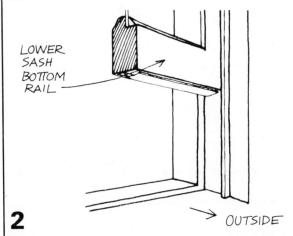

2

Install strips the full width of the sash on the bottom of the lower sash bottom rail and the top of the upper sash top rail.

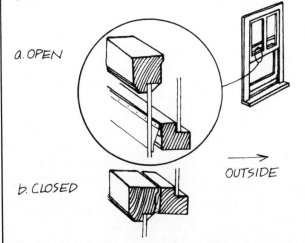

Then attach a strip the full width of the window to the upper sash bottom rail. Countersink the nails slightly so they won't catch on the lower sash top rail.

Rolled vinyl

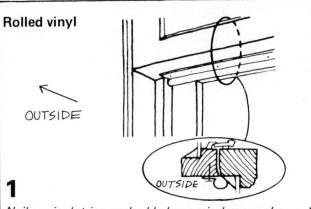

1

Nail on vinyl strips on double-hung windows as shown. A sliding window is much the same and can be treated as a double-hung window turned on its side. Casement and

2

Tilting windows should be weatherstripped with the vinyl nailed to the window casing so that, as the window shuts, it compresses the roll.

Adhesive-backed foam strip

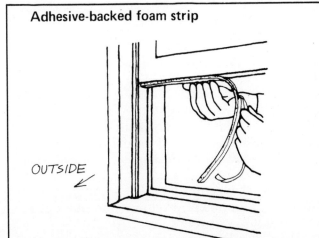

Install adhesive backed foam, on all types of windows, only where there is no friction. On double-hung windows, this is only on the bottom (as shown) and top rails. Other types of windows can use foam strips in many more places.

Leaded or Stained Glass Windows

Unless you are really committed to doing your own repair work it might be best to leave leaded or stained glass windows to the experts. They are very tricky, and in the case of antique windows a great deal of beauty can be lost by making a small mistake.

Minor repairs can be done to the lead by using a soldering iron, just one of the little electric gun types, with resin core solder. Just apply the heat and solder simultaneously, and once the solder has filled the hole or dent back off *instantly*.

If you are attempting repair of a broken out piece, first carefully take out all the broken glass and reconstruct the broken piece on some cardboard. Make a template and take it to a glass cutter for a replacement piece. Also take some of the glass with you for a sample of the proper color.

Then use a pair of wire cutters—diagonal cutters, dikes—to snip the leaded portion of the window as shown in the illustration.

Fold all these little pieces of lead up and out and put in the new piece of glass. Then fold them back down over the glass, ever so gently, and use the soldering gun to heat and fill all the little cracks where the wire cutter went through.

It is really very difficult and not recommended for any except the totally committed or desperate.

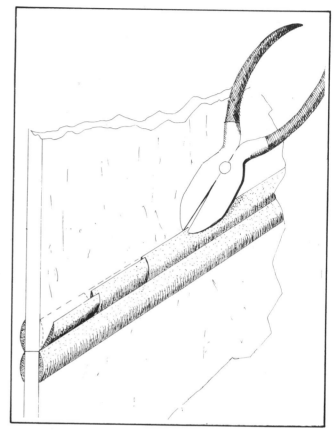

Procedure for repairing leaded glass: Cut the lead strips as shown with tinsnips or wirecutters. Then fold back and up and remove broken glass. After new glass is installed fold pieces back and solder lightly on cuts.

Sticking Windows

An added point on old windows with wooden frames: although not strictly a repair, windows that stick and will not open are an irritation that deserves mention.

Usually the reason is excessive painting and repainting of the windows so they are actually too big—with the added layers of paint—to move easily in the frame. In other cases the cause is humidity that makes the wood swell. For either situation the repair is the same.

Pull the slider strips off—they are much like the stops on a permanent window—and pull out the whole window, with frame.

Then use a non-filling rasp to take some wood off from the outside—say a full sixteenth off each side—and then put the window back, using the same holes for the nails.

It will slide easily from then on, or until the next thirty-six layers of paint have accumulated.

Screens

Screen repair is almost unbelievable, because it is not only an easy job that does not cost much and looks good when you are done, but it can even be fun.

The type of repair depends naturally on the type of screen. Before getting down to specifics a word about screen material.

Most people use metal screen but you will also find plastic, especially on sliding glass doors and other large applications. To be sure, plastic screening will not rust, which is a very big plus. Metal screens, especially in coastal areas, seem to rust out as fast as you get them in. But plastic screens have not been really perfected yet, and they seem to stretch with the heat of the sun and weather. It is almost impossible to keep plastic screens from looking slightly tired and baggy; the more so if you have got children or pets that run into the screens.

In either case, the repair method is the same, but your choice of materials should be carefully studied before you begin the repair.

Wood Screens

All around the outside edge and across the middle you will find small nailing strips of wood which hold the screen material on. Using a claw hammer or wide screwdriver, pry the strips off and remove all the nails. They will be rusty and you might as well throw them away and buy new ½-inch galvanized brads for replacement. But remember how the strips came off or make a list, so you can put them back in *exactly* the same order.

Now lay your screen material on the frame and cut the screening the right size so that it just slightly overlaps the nailing strips.

Cut the screening with either a very good and tight set of tinsnips, or a very poor set of scissors you do not care about.

When the new piece is cut, put the nailing strips back on, stretching the screen material a little so it is tight. Do not pull it hard, just firmly, and nail the strips on six inch centers. Do the top and bottom first, then the sides, then the middle.

As an aid to getting the screening in the right place some people use a heavy duty stapler, the kind used on insulation, and tack the screening in place all around before nailing down the strips. It is not mandatory but it helps, particularly if your thumbs seem to get in your way.

Also, while you are repairing the screens it is a good time to check the tightness of the frames. Examine the corners for looseness. If there is a problem get some metal corner-brackets (the little L-shaped things) and screw then in place with short wood screws. A touch of glue in the corners does not hurt, and will help hold until your regular maintenance program comes around.

Aluminum Frame Screening

Not as strong as wood screens, aluminum screens really amount to a small metal frame with a kind of rubber strip that runs all around.

It is better to replace with plastic screening, because it is the only material pliable enough to insert into the little groove and still allow the rubber strip to fit correctly into the slot.

Cut the screening big enough to overlap the groove ⅛ inch or so, and lay it across the frame in position. Then put the plastic strip over it and press it in all around, a bit at a time, gently pressing the strip in place with the fingers.

Do not worry if the frame feels loose and wobbly, even with the screen on tight. Aluminum screen

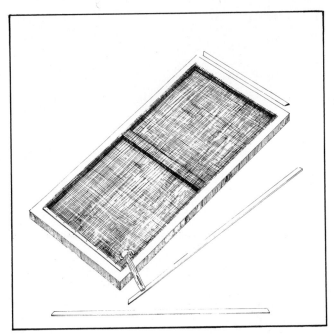

Additional nailing strips go all the way around the perimeter.

frames are not particularly rigid and get their strength from the larger window frame once in place.

Also, do not stretch the screening as you put it on. The screen will be taken up by the tube and groove when you press it down, which will adequately stretch the material.

Screen Doors and Sliders

Essentially, fixing screen doors is exactly the same as fixing windows, but more so. Wooden screen doors have nailing strips, the same as wooden windows, and metal sliding doors have the plastic strip and groove, as do aluminum windows. Just cut the material the right size and use the same method as you would use with a window.

If you have a wooden screen door without a wire with a turnbuckle to keep it tight, this might be a good time to put one in. Just buy a turnbuckle kit at the nearest hardware and put it in diagonally from top to bottom; instructions come with the kit. Do not overtighten, but make it snug and it will keep the door from sagging.

Also, if you have pets or children, you might as well install a plywood (¼ inch) screen on the bottom half of the door. Tack it to the screen nailing strips on the outside and it will keep your screen from getting torn out. . .for awhile. Nothing is impervious to children and pets forever.

Quick Fixes

Often a cut will hit a screen on the hottest night of the year, at the height of mosquito season or just when the hardware store will be closed all weekend. There is no way to predict this, but it happens often enough to be the rule.

If this happens to you, or if you just can't get screening, you might try "sewing" the damaged area.

Simply take some thin wire—a single strand from picture-hanging wire, unbraided from the rest, works very well—and patch the cut by working the

wire back and forth through the screen to sew up the tear or cut.

If you do not have any wire, thread will get the job done on a temporary basis so you can keep the window open and the bugs out.

A final thought on screening. As this is being written many of the discount stores are offering screen repair kits and the like. They get the job done. You buy precut screening according to your window size and put it in. But if you own a home, savings can be substantial by purchasing a whole roll of screening material and keeping it stored in the basement or storage area.

As easy as it is to work with, you take very little extra time by cutting it to fit yourself. In this case, the gimmick of a kit saves you nothing and costs more money than it is worth.

Drapery Ripout Repair

One of the more common problems with the recurring fashion demand for wide and heavy draperies is that they keep pulling out of the wall.

The repair is relatively simple. Whether drywall or lath and plaster, use the expanding wing nut—the kind with wings which open up when they get past the wall surface—or a "molly" to rehang the drapery rod. This will usually take care of the problem. If not, alongside each edge of the window (and it *has* to be there for structural purposes) you will find a stud. Use a 3 inch wood screw with thread all the way, and a round head with wide washers, to screw the drapery rod holder to the wall. It will not pull out again.

chapter seven

doors

Most people wait until their doors refuse to open or close before they worry about their repair. Steps should be taken long before this stage is reached, however, because poorly functioning doors can cause a great deal of unnecessary frustrations. A door that sticks so that you must jerk it open can have you jerking every door you come to for weeks.

A good maintenance program will catch most door problems before they become destructive, but if you are buying a new or old place or did not start your program in time to catch the problems, below are listed common door ailments and their cures.

Finishes

Weathered External Doors

A common problem in older homes that have been neglected, weathered-out doors are particularly sad because they are often those beautiful old paneled doors which you simply cannot replace.

Of course after a certain point, once the panels are completely cracked out, there is very little you can do except replace the door. But if the weathering is not too extensive and the cracking has not decimated the wood completely, there are some measures you can try.

First, take the door off and clean it as well as you can, working with a wire brush. Once it is clean, rub it with linseed oil, even if it had been painted; this will get into the cracks and stabilize the shrinkage.

Then work a filler into the door, all over—a good tight filler—and sand when dry. Do not be afraid to oversand because what you are working for is a smooth surface. Finally, paint with a top-quality enamel, working in several thin coats rather than one thick one. And do not rehang the door until the paint is totally dry and cured out which could be as long as two days. You want the wood to be well protected before subjecting the door to normal work.

Hinges

Rotted Out Exterior Hinges

Another common problem with older homes occurs when weather rots out the hinges: rough weather and damaging elements work back up under the hinge plates and soak the wood until it rots.

Repair is difficult, but not impossible. First remove the door, and the hinges, and clean and pick everything out of the damaged areas under the hinge plates. Use a screwdriver to pick the rotten wood out—all of it.

With everything clean, mix up some epoxy glue—the kind that comes in two tubes—and dip the non-striking ends of matches into the glue and poke them down into the old screw holes; leave them in there, with plenty of glue on them. They will glue themselves in tightly, and you should jam as many into each hole as will fit, on both the door (if it is rotted out) and the frame. Just let them stick out for the moment; you can cut them off later when the glue is good and dry.

Now, wearing rubber gloves, "fill" all the torn out wood spots with epoxy, mashing it well in at first so it sticks, then leveling it off to meet the level of the wood. What you are doing, in effect, is rebuilding the wood with epoxy, reconstructing the rotted-out portions.

When the epoxy is well set—at least 24 hours—break off the matches and file or sand everything down so that it is even and smooth.

Then drill small pilot holes and screw the hinges back in place and rehang the door exactly as it was, taking care to tighten all screws snugly, but not with massive torque which could strip them out.

This repair should last as long as the original wood; if the problem reoccurs, repeat the procedure.

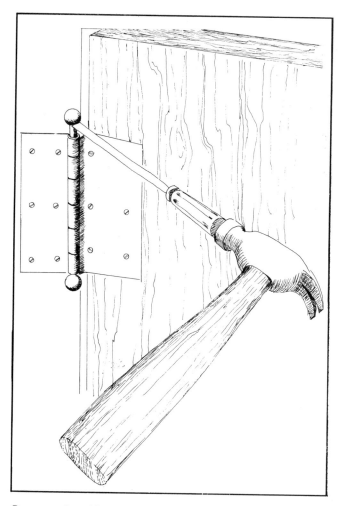

Remove door hinges.

Stripped Out Hinge Screws

As already explained, fill out the holes by dipping wooden matches liberally into epoxy, jamming them into the holes. Let dry, and cure well. When thoroughly set, break off matches flush, file or sand, and drill small pilot hole and rehang.
Note. If you have no epoxy or glue handy, sometimes a simple wooden match jammed into the hole and broken off will do the job temporarily.

Squeaky Hinges

Oil, of course, cures squeaky hinges. But oil can be messy and smelly and to avoid the petroleum stink you might try vegetable oil, which works well; or, for a lasting cure pull the hinge pins and wipe them lightly with petroleum jelly. It will last for months or even years, with never a sound.

Loose Hinges

When hinges are very old, or have had excessive use, they will often wear themselves "loose" around the hinge pins—the holes actually get larger. The best solution is to replace the whole hinge. But sometimes old hinges are beautiful, and cannot be replaced.

Still, you cannot have doors rattling and wobbling every time you open them; the cure is to pull the hinge plates and "compress" the pin holes slightly in a vise. Not too much pressure here, just a tiny bit for each of the little hinge pin holes, on both plates for each hinge.

Then wipe the hinge pin with petroleum jelly and put it all back together. The hinges will last for another five years or so, and should be as tight as new hinges.

Locksets

Replacing Locksets

Work with the door open, and look all around the knob until you find a little spring slotted lock—just an edge of metal. This you can push in with a knifeblade and it will release the knob. You then pull the knob off and the whole lockset assembly will be exposed. (All this will be on the interior side of the house or locked room, if the lockset was installed correctly in the first place.)

Two screws will go all the way through the door to hold the assembly in place. Take them both all the way out, then pull the assembly out from both sides.

Now go to the edge of the door and you will find two small wood screws holding the actual latching mechanism in place. Remove them and pull the latch out.

Installation of the new lockset is a simple reversal of the procedure: screw the latch in first, then put the lockset assembly in—with the key portion, facing the outside. And that is all there is to it except for one vital consideration: with all the burglary going on, and increasing at such a drastic rate, remember that a lockset merely keeps the door closed, and is not adequate to stop entry. It is so easily slipped open that even children can pop a lockset.

Nor are chain slide locks secure for anything other than mental reassurance. Anybody can kick a door open and tear off the chain lock in the process.

Most authorities advise that for relative security you need a shot-bolt kind of system, either the over-and-down manual or key-driven bolt that actually

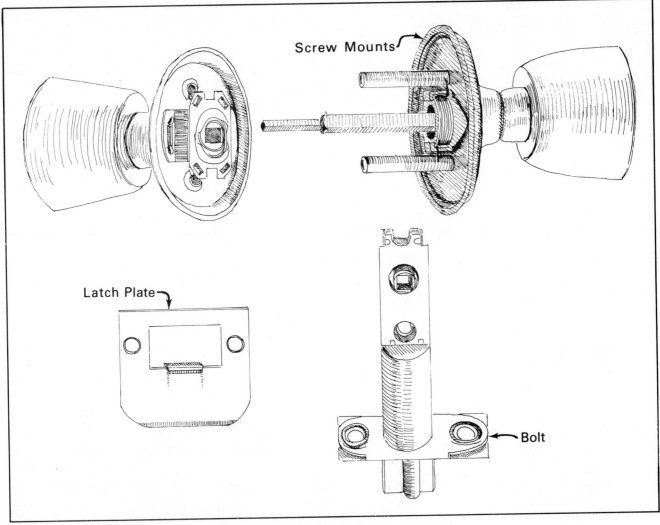

Just follow the instructions on the new lockset, or study the old before replacing it. They look much more complicated than they really are. Shown above are lockset components.

goes from the door over *into* the door frame and seats in metal.

Installing such a bolt lock set is easy—they come with precut templates and complete instructions. This perhaps does not come under a "repair" heading. But if you have ever had your home violated— and that's how it feels—and your possessions stolen, putting in a bolt set just might be considered a necessary repair.

Rough-Working Locksets

Especially with newer homes, but now and then with older homes, the locksets will work only with difficulty and require much key wiggling.

The classic fix for this is to squirt a bit of graphite lubricant into the keyhole; usually it will work well enough. But if along with the graphite you take some steel wool and work the teeth on the keyhole down so they are not rough, you will find that it works much better.

Freeing Up Old Locksets

A major problem with old homes is that their truly beautiful locksets—sometimes of ornate bronze, or sculpted leaf patterns—do not work. They have rusted or corroded into uselessness.

Of course for security purposes, as already discussed, you should put in a decent shot bolt system

installing a new lock

a. Remove worn out, broken, or low-security lock.
b. Remove latch of old lock.
c. Use template packed with new lock to mark area to be enlarged.
d. If a jig is available (as shown), use hole saw to enlarge area to accept new lock mechanism.
e. If hole requires only minor enlargement use a wood rasp or similar tool.

f. Cut away excess wood in edge of door, if necessary, to accommodate new latch plate.
g. Install latch.
h. Insert lock mechanism from outside of door.
i. Attach mounting plate on outside of door and snap on trim and knob.

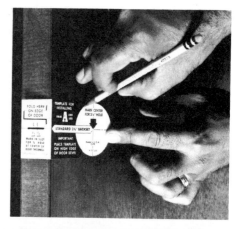

anyway. But even so, it is sometimes nice to have the old one work—at least the latch part, if only for looks.

The best way to free up the lockset is to remove it and clean off the dirt or rust. First take the knobs off, then the pull-out square rod that holds the knobs, and finally the two cover plates. Soak the whole thing in some loosening-solvent product that you can buy in any hardware store. Let it soak for a few days, until all the rust and dirt has loosened, and all the screws and pieces work easily. Then rinse it in thin motor oil, let it hang for another day, wipe it well with clean dry rags, and put it back on the door exactly the same as it came out. Some of those old sets were virtually custom-made for the door; often they will only fit one way, with the screws going back on exactly as they came out.

Note. Do not drown everything up with oil. Be sure it has been wiped well before installing because the oil will stain the door around the lockset.

Too Tight or Too Loose?

Sticking Doors

The most common door problem is sticking; the door that jams and will not open without that extra tug is especially frustrating.

Causes. There are several reasons for a door sticking, and because of that you should do nothing when a door first begins to stick. You must further evaluate the situation.

The cause of the door's sticking might be critical. Often, for instance, doors stick because humidity has risen and caused the wood to swell. This problem is easily fixed, as will be discussed shortly. If it is due to temporary ambient weather—a rainstorm that has moved in or a pressure system bringing a sudden and unusual increase in humidity—leave the door alone. The condition will pass and the door will return to normal.

Now and again, however, the sticking door merely signals some other underlying problem. If the house sags, for example, it can throw out door frames all over the house. The first indication you will have is the sudden sticking of doors where they once moved freely.

So if a door or doors begin to stick, prowl the house—in the basement beneath the sticking door if possible—to see if there is any other evidence of sag …split boards, cracked drywall or plaster. It is still treatable even if it *is* a sagging wall (caused by water problems, termites, rot), but you should know the condition and cause of the difficulty before attempt-

ing repair. If it *is* sag, go to the chapter on "Aging Problems" to correct the difficulty.

Finally, if the house does not sag and the humidity has not suddenly risen, still do not take action until you check the door frame. The frames of the door may have shrunk, pulled in from their nails, and effectively made the doorway smaller.

Cure for Shrunken Frame. Take a hammer and, using a buffer board to pound on while keeping the door open, go down both sides of the doorway opening, pounding the jamb outwards, stopping to pound every six inches or so.

If the door moves freely after this, take some 10d finishing nails and nail the jamb firmly in position. Then set the nails and fill the holes with a stick of appropriately colored nail filler material. These sticks are sold at most lumber yards and hardware stores.

Cure for Permanent High Humidity. If your home has reoccurring high humidity—due for example to a new humidifier or plants in the room—and the door is likely to stay swollen, it will have to be pulled and wood taken off.

Here again, it is best to stay away from the time-honored method. For decades, any time a door has stuck, the homeowner has jerked it down and planed a bit off the edge to make it fit. Well, this will work. But planes are tricky; if the blade is set wrong or you hit the grain wrong it is possible to mar the edge of the door.

It is better to set the door up on edge and use a non-filling wood rasp to take off about a sixteenth of an inch. The rasp will not "run away" with you and split the wood out; it will just take off a little with each sweep, and leave you in control.

Take off a touch more than you think you will need to take off, to make it loose; then paint or varnish the edge of the door to match and rehang the door, using sticks or pencils to hold it in position (see illustration on p. 45).

Shrunken Door Panels

Almost the opposite of the swelling, sticking door, shrinking usually occurs with new panelled doors; these panels can shrink a great deal. The cause is too green a wood used in construction, a side effect of trying to produce homes as quickly and therefore as cheaply as possible. It is not uncommon to find bare wood showing around a painted panel. This strip can be as much as a ¼ inch, and can be pretty unsightly.

Unfortunately there is no way to "cure" the problem, short of returning the door to the manufacturer.

All you can do is paint the offending strip of wood to match using paint or stain. And if the panel has become loose, so it rattles in its slot, squirt just a little glue back into the crack; the white glue in the squeeze bottle will take care of it admirably.

Separation of Corners

One of the primary problems with older doors is that the members come apart. The glue dries out; the weather comes in; the door literally begins to fall apart.

Take the door down, but not apart, work a good wood glue deeply into the seams between the members and press them back together. Take a piece of inexpensive hemp rope ½ inch in diameter, and make a tourniquet clamp as illustrated.

When the wood has been tightened enough to be firm and squeeze the glue out, wipe excess glue off and tie or tape the stick of your clamp in position until the glue is well dried.

Do not try to hurry this process. Let the glue dry completely, perhaps for a couple of days, before rehanging the door.

Latches

Stripped Out Latch Screws

As with hinge screws, the screws holding the latch set in the door or wall can strip out. Mix up a little epoxy and jam it back into the hole with a wooden match.

When the epoxy is well set (some of the new so-

called five minute epoxies are very good for this), break the matches off flush and sand level before re-screwing the latch back in.

Rotted-Out Latch Assemblies

Older homes frequently will have the latch assemblies rotted out of the exterior doors due to bad weather and poor maintenance.

As an alternative to replacing the door (since that is expensive and often it will be impossible to find a new door as suited to the house as the old one) you

Let door rest on floor using pencils as spacers and supports.

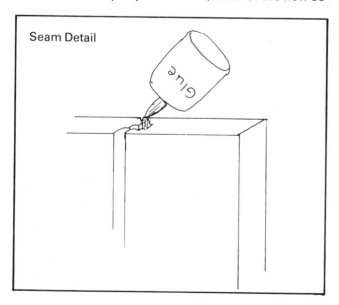

can "rebuild" the latch hole and make it serve for years.

Start with rubber gloves, and then mix a putty of epoxy and wood sanding dust. Mix it with a flat knife or wooden match and keep adding sanding dust until you have a thickish putty that will hold a shape. You can get the sanding dust by sanding a soft pine scrap with coarse sandpaper.

Once the putty has thickened and the latch assembly has been removed from the door, clean out all split and rotted wood from the hole. Rebuild it to the orginal shape using the epoxy-wood putty.

Do not use quick-dry epoxy; use the slow stuff and take your time. Just fill and push so that the epoxy works well back into the damaged wood, and build it out until the repair job approximates the orig-inal shape. Then let it cure for two or three days; really let it set up before replacing the lockset.

Note. All pilot holes for screws should be drilled smaller than if you were using natural wood, but do not worry about holding power—the epoxy will hold well because the wood sandings give it tensile strength. Also, we attempted to fix a rotted door using premixed fiberglass putty; theoretically it would work well for this application. But it did not turn out well at all; the material seemed too brittle.

Doors That Will Not Latch

After a time some doors stop latching correctly; old doors kind of half catch, then swing open.

The cause is age again—the casing shrinks until the latch plate in the casing actually moves too far away from the door for the latch to engage it properly. What you have to do, obviously, is move the latch plate back over so the latch will catch it and lock.

There are several ways of doing this, including shimming out with wood, as most people do. But if you take an old piece of thick boot leather, cut it the same size as the latch plate and put it beneath the plate for a shim, not only will you find it easier to use than wood but it will not split out.

Trim off any excess with a razor blade and touch up the edge of leather with appropriate paint or varnish. (The leather takes stain and looks like wood when you are finished.)

General Problems

Rehanging Doors

Putting a door back on after repairing it is relatively simple if you do not try to lift the whole door by one corner.

Put some pencils or pieces of wood of the same thickness across the door jamb, as in the sketch, and rehanging the door will be easy.

Screws Coming Loose

Because of heavy use—doors moving all the time, slamming, jarring—wood screws often work loose. When this happens, pull them and give them a covering of glue. Then screw them back in while the glue is still wet, and it should solve the problem.

Screw the rope tight enough to squeeze out excess glue, but not so tight that the rope breaks.

weatherstrip your doors

an easy do-it-yourself project

You can weatherstrip your doors even if you're not an experienced handyman. There are several types of weatherstripping for doors, each with its own level of effectiveness, durability and degree of installation difficulty. Select among the options given the one you feel is best for you. *The installations are the same for the two sides and top of a door,* with a different, more durable one for the threshold.

the alternative methods and materials

1. Adhesive backed foam:

Tools

Knife or shears,
Tape measure

Evaluation—*extremely easy to install, invisible when installed, not very durable, more effective on doors than windows.*

Installation—*stick foam to inside face of jamb.*

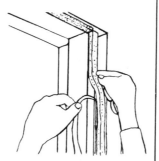

2. Rolled vinyl with aluminum channel backing:

Tools

Hammer, nails,
Tin snips
Tape measure

Evaluation—*easy to install, visible when installed, durable.*

Installation—*nail strip snugly against door on the casing.*

3. Foam rubber with wood backing:

Tools

Hammer, nails,
Hand saw,
Tape measure

Evaluation—*easy to install, visible when installed, not very durable.*

Installation—*nail strip snugly against the closed door. Space nails 8 to 12 inches apart.*

4. Spring metal:

Tools

Tin snips
Hammer, nails,
Tape measure

Evaluation—*easy to install, invisible when installed, extremely durable.*

Installation—*cut to length and tack in place. Lift outer edge of strip with screwdriver after tacking, for better seal.*

Note: *These methods are harder than 1 through 4.*

5. Interlocking metal channels:

Tools

*Hack saw,
Hammer, nails,
Tape measure*

Evaluation—*difficult to install (alignment is critical), visible when installed, durable but subject to damage, because they're exposed, excellent seal.*

Installation—*cut and fit strips to head of door first: male strip on door, female on head; then hinge side of door: male strip on jamb, female on door; finally lock side on door, female on jamb.*

6. Fitted interlocking metal channels: (J-Strips)

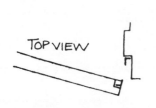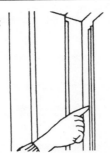

Evaluation—*very difficult to install, exceptionally good weather seal, invisible when installed, not exposed to possible damage.*

Installation—*should be installed by a carpenter. Not appropriate for do-it-yourself installation unless done by an accomplished handyman.*

7. Sweeps:

Tools

*Screwdriver,
Hack saw,
Tape measure*

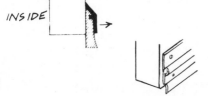

Evaluation—*useful for flat threshholds, may drag on carpet or rug.*

Installation—*cut sweep to fit 1/16 inch in from the edges of the door. Some sweeps are installed on the inside and some outside. Check instructions for your particular type.*

Source: Dept. of Housing and Urban Development.

8. Door Shoes:

Tools

*Screwdriver,
Hack saw,
Plane,
Tape measure*

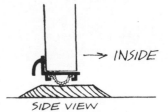

Evaluation—*useful with wooden threshhold that is not worn, very durable, difficult to install (must remove door).*

Installation—*remove door and trim required amount off bottom. Cut to door width. Install by sliding vinyl out and fasten with screws.*

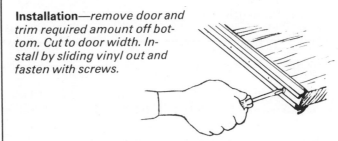

9. Vinyl bulb threshhold:

Tools

*Screwdriver,
Hack saw,
Plane,
Tape measure*

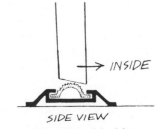

Evaluation—*useful where there is no threshhold or wooden one is worn out, difficult to install, vinyl will wear but replacements are available.*

Installation—*remove door and trim required amount off bottom. Bottom should have about 1/8'' bevel to seal against vinyl. Be sure bevel is cut in right direction for opening.*

10. Interlocking threshhold:

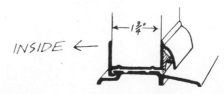

Evalualtion–*very difficult to install, exceptionally good weather seal.*

Installation–*should be installed by a skilled carpenter.*

Sliding Doors

Rough Track Movement

Almost all problems with sliding doors come down to dirty tracks.

Any time a sliding door does not work properly, first check the bottom slide track for obstructions. Usually you will find something jammed into the track as though it had been welded there.

If the bottom track is clear, check the top for possible obstructions. If both tracks are clear, check the wheel adjustment screws located at the bottom corners. They sometimes vibrate loose with use and allow the door to "settle" too far down on the track for easy movement.

If the tracks are not obstructed, and the screws have not come loose, check to see if the house is settling. On a span as wide as a sliding glass door a little settling in the middle can have a very noticeable effect on the door movement. A half inch or so can warp the frame so badly the door will be almost impossible to open or close.

If the house has settled check the chapter on "Aging" for possible repairs. Do not try to adjust the door enough to compensate for a continuing sag; you will not be able to keep up with the sag and the effect will be that the doors look crooked and strange.

Rough Latches

It is almost impossible to find a sliding glass door with a latch that *does* work correctly.

To repair, fill the offending latch with graphite lubricant and pray for the best. Generally, over a period of time and with additional use and graphite, the action will smooth out. With sliding door systems the way they are now, that is about all you can hope for. Replacing the door may solve it, but the percentages are that a new door will also have a rough-working latch. New sliding glass doors can be bought in pre-assembled packages with complete instructions for homeowner installation.

chapter eight

plumbing & water appliances

Major repair of catastrophic plumbing problems—when replumbing of a whole house is necessary due to pipe rot, for example—is very difficult and should not be attempted without a thorough knowledge of both the tools and the materials. It demands strength and is dirty work; unless you are stone broke it might be better to hire it done.

With the question of major problems out of the way it might be salient to point out that in *all* other cases repairs are simple, if sometimes a bit noxious, and are within reach of the homeowner. If a certain degree of care is taken the home repair will be of professional quality.

Drains

Far and away the most common problem in plumbing, the stopped drain is a lesson in plumbing methodology—almost a march through the spectrum of repair methods.

First, try the plunger. Push down and pull up with surging action to try to blow a "plug" of water through the stopped area. Usually this will work. After the drain is cleared, run very hot water through it. Often the plug will be of grease or sludge buildup and hot water will melt the grease out and completely clean the pipe. (Aside from television ads, no

PLUMBING TROUBLE-SHOOTING CHART
DRAINS

Symptoms	Main drain backup	Main drain, yard	Clogged traps	Using plunger	Using wire	Using snake	Using hose, Bsmt.	Septic system	Treating clogged drain at same level
Sink backing up		X	X	X	X			X	
Tub backing up			X	X	X			X	
Toilet backing up	X			X					X
Water backing up in Bsmt.	X	X			X	X	X		
Water backing up (seepage) in yard	X						X		
Water backing up (dripping) in Bsmt. ceiling		X						X	
Water in upstairs floor								X	
Water under cabinets in kitchen/bathroom		X						X	
Seepage (dampness) around house		X						X	
Turn to repair info on . . .	Main drain backup	Main drain, yard	Clogged traps	Using plunger	Using wire	Using snake	Using hose, Bsmt.	Septic system	Treating clogged drain at same level

consistent success is apparent using various drain cleaning agents, either liquid or granular. On a maintenance basis they may work, but for clearing a really stopped drain they never seem to get the job done.)

If the plunger does not work, go to the easiest access point—down through the sink drain or toilet—with a long piece of wire. It is possible the plug area is close by and the wire will work through. Again, if the wire clears the drain, run hot water through it and bore it out.

If the wire does not work, use a snake—the wire-coil kind used by plumbers. They are easy to rent, if you do not own one or know where to borrow one. Work the snake into the easiest access point that is relatively straight, do not go through the trap, but below the trap once it has been removed. The less bends you have to negotiate, the better. As for the method, wear gloves and almost gently work the snake down to the stopped point, then back and forth until you break through. Never force anything, but move back and forth, back and forth, until the resis-

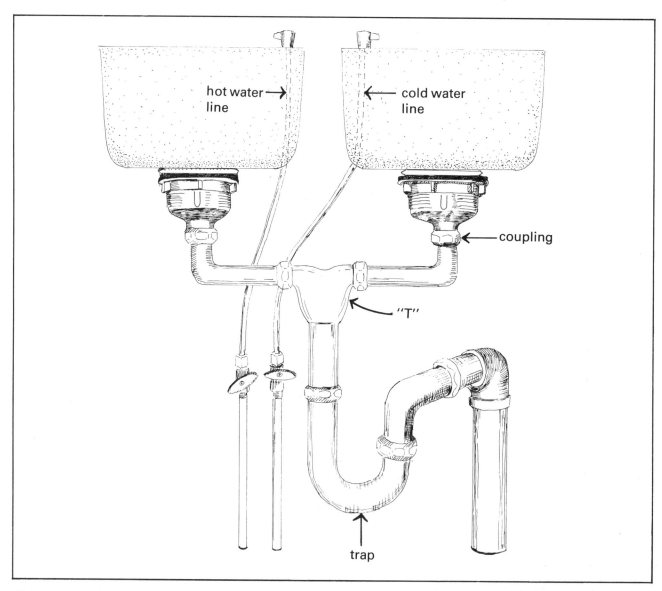

hot water line

cold water line

coupling

"T"

trap

Fixing pipes or drains is not as scary as it looks.

tance is gone. If you just keep pushing the plug blockage—and in an old house it could be fifteen feet of solid materials—it will just compact and form a more solid front. You must allow the snake to find a way through, a bit at a time. And once again, when the drain is cleared run hot water through to further open it.

Leaking Drains

In plumbing problems a leak almost always means either a broken pipe or loose joint. Under-sink leaks are the most common and they usually come from traps. The most common cause of traps that leak is their old and tired ring-washers at the joints. Repair is easy, but messy. Use a large pipe wrench and loosen the big nuts at either end of the trap—after placing a pot or bucket to catch the inevitable water. Wiggle and pull the trap out of place and remove the mashed washers around the ends. (They will be almost flat, and maybe torn.) Then take them down to the local hardware, buy new ones, and put the whole assembly back together. When retightening the nuts do not go overboard with the wrench. You can develop a lot of torque with a large pipe wrench and the threads are easy to strip. Just get it snug-tight and let it go at that.

If the source of the drain leak is not in the trap, but is further down the line, the repair depends on the kind of pipe. If you have threaded, galvanized pipe for a drain system (probable if your house is older), take a large pipe wrench, adjust it to fit tight until the teeth will bite in, and tighten the leaking pipe a quarter turn. Use plenty of force. Old pipes are very hard to move. But do not overdo it—a drip-leak will be cured with just a little tightening: all that is necessary is enough pressure to recompress the loosened threads inside the pipe. The leak comes when corrosion slightly erodes the threads and allows a trickle of water to work through; the slightest tightening will stop the leak and retighten the corroded spot.

If the leaking drain comes from a plastic pipe, more common in newer homes, just put a dab of plastic pipe adhesive at the leak point. Allow it to dry for a few minutes before using it. If you do not have any plastic pipe adhesive, model airplane cement will do the job.

Very rarely a drain leak will occur in a copper drain pipe. This is rare because copper is very expensive and not often used in drains. If a leak occurs at a solder joint, use a small propane torch to heat the leak area. Heat just until the solder begins to flow, then instantly remove the heat. It is not necessary to add solder; just heat the existing solder to fill the gap.

The final drain leak covered here occurs around a cast pipe, usually in the basement, where the pipe goes down the wall or into the floor. Here the packing might come loose around a joint where two sections of cast pipe come together. Take a screwdriver and hammer and repack the joint as shown in the sketch. This leak is uncommon because the packing does not usually come loose, and even if it does the leak will not show unless a plug backs the drain up enough to force the water back out.

In all drain leak problems, try not to hurry. Often, especially in small drip-leaks or seepage problems, the drain will fix itself.

Pipes

Dripping Faucet

One of the most common leak problems is the dripping faucet. Usually, the drip occurs when the rubber washer in the tip of the assembly wears

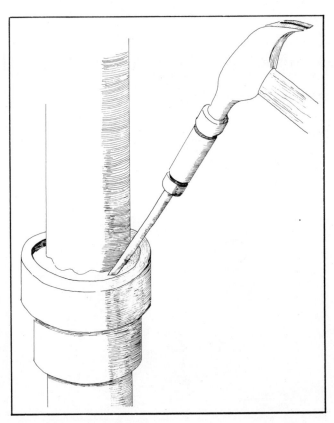

Drive the lead and packing down hard to seal the joint, then look for the cause of the drain backing up to stop the joint leak at its source.

down; the washer is on the faucet handle, held onto the end by a little screw. (See sketch.) So go to the hardware store and buy an assorted box of rubber faucet washers, just to have on hand, and make sure you have a small pipe wrench and a good screwdriver.

Under the sink you will find two secondary gate valves—faucet handles—and you first turn these off. This prevents additional water from coming into the pipe. Then you turn the leaking faucets on, to release pressure, and when you are sure no water is left in the pipes because no more water is running, remove

The washer is at the very bottom of everything. One nice feature is that faucets usually come apart easily because they are used so much.

the faucet handle. You will note that the faucet is held down in the housing by a standard collar-nut (see sketch). Use the pipe wrench to loosen this nut, by turning it counterclockwise, and when it has been removed the faucet core will lift out of the housing as illustrated. On the bottom of the faucet core there is a rubber washer; take the screw out and replace it with the right-sized washer from the assorted washer box. Then reverse the process, putting the core back in, the collar-nut on and the handle back on. The leak will have stopped dripping.

Galvanized-Pipe Leaks

Seep-drip leaks in exposed pipes, as with drain repair, depend on the type of pipe. If the leaking pipes are galvanized, just tighten the leaking joint a hair with a pipe wrench (not over a quarter turn). As with drains, the threads rust and corrode; if you just re-compress them a bit the leak is fixed.

Nongalvanized-Pipe Leaks

Whenever the pipe does not have threaded joints the pipe should be drained of water for repair of a slow or seeping leak.

Find the main gate valve for the house. Somewhere in the basement, crawlspace or just outside, there will be a single faucet handle that cuts off water to the whole house. Turn the water off with this main valve, then open the lowest faucet (in the basement) in the house and allow all the water in the pipes to drain down and out. Also open up an upstairs faucet to allow air to bleed down into the pipe when the water runs out; this will insure a thorough drain.

With the pipes drained, the fix can be initiated. If the leak is plastic, work some plastic adhesive into the hole and allow it to dry well—for over an hour—before putting pressure on the pipe again. Unlike drain situations, here there will be a goodly amount of pressure, perhaps forty to sixty psi, so be sure the fix has taken effect before restoring water.

If the slow leak is in copper pipe, the most common in relatively recent homes, the first step is the same. Turn off the water, drain all the pipes, then use a propane torch to heat the leaking joint to allow the solder to reform. As with drains it is not necessary to apply more solder; just barely melt what is already there and let it reharden.

Finally, discussing slow leaks, be sure that the problem is indeed a leak. Sometimes a change in at-

PLUMBING TROUBLE-SHOOTING CHART
LEAKS

Symptoms	Replacing faucet washer	Stopping leak with epoxied screw	Condensation	Leak repairs	Main faucet repacking	Shutting water at main in Bsmt.
Faucet drip	X					
Dampness on floor			X	X		
Spray leak		X		X		X
Flow leak		X		X		X
Seep leak			X	X		
Burst leak				X		X
"Puddling" around faucet mount	X				X	

Turn to repair info on . . .

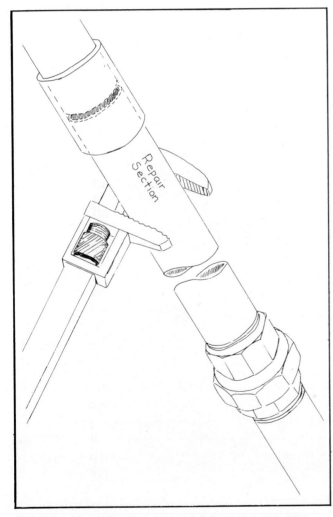

Use plenty of heft when wrenching loose galvanized pipes. They are usually nearly welded shut with rust and age.

Joining DWV Plastic Pipe can be accomplished in just a few steps with a brush. First, the bed of the plastic pipe socket is brushed with a cleaning agent (A); same is done for the outer rim of the pipe to be inserted (B). Next, a special welding solvent is brushed on the pipe rim (C) and inner side of the socket (D). The joint is then completed by simply inserting the pipe in the fitting Socket (E) with a tightening, twisting motion.

Sockets are provided on all fittings, which come in a full range of types including a splicing collar. Plastic pipe comes in plain 10 foot lengths, and is cut to proper length for use with an ordinary carpenter's handsaw.

mospheric conditions will cause a pipe to "sweat" and leave a few drops. Be certain the leak is leaking, and that the pipe is not just shedding a bit of condensation.

Burst Pipes

Generally caused by freezing, and most often in hot-water heating systems which have been left untended for a few days or weeks, burst pipes can involve extended household damage if not caught immediately.

A frozen pipe will stay plugged until it melts out. But once it melts and starts to allow water to flow, the leak may ruin walls, ceilings and floors.

The repair need not be costly if caught in time. First, obviously, you must turn off the source of water. As quickly as you find the burst pipe, turn off the main water to the house and open a lower faucet or drain to relieve the pressure on the broken area.

When all water is drained out of the pipe, a further evaluation is necessary. Specific repair methods depend on the kind of pipe involved.

If galvanized, use a large pipe wrench to break loose and unscrew the section of pipe that has burst. Take out the whole piece, even if it is long. Remember that it unscrews like a regular bolt: counterclockwise to loosen, clockwise to tighten. Before breaking it loose find the nearest coupling joint (see sketch) and release that end at the coupling by unscrewing it. Holding the burst piece of galvanized pipe, go to the local plumbing supply or hardware and get a piece of new pipe that is cut to the right length and threaded the same as the one you have taken out. While you are there pick up a tube of pipe compound to smear on the threads.

Back at the house, smear all the threads with the pipe compound and rebuild the damaged section of pipe with the new pipe making everything as tight as you can. When you think the pipe is repaired turn the water on and see what happens. There might be a small seep leak. If so, just tighten a little to further compress the threads and swage the goop in.

If the burst pipe is plastic, the repair is unbelievably easy. After the water system is turned off and drained, cut out the broken piece of tubing with a hacksaw. Then get a new, exactly-the-same-size piece from the hardware and a couple of slip-couplings plus a small can of plastic pipe adhesive. First put the couplings on the two ends of the cut off pipes in the wall, gluing them liberally and allowing the glue to dry. Then put a good coat of glue on both ends of the new piece of pipe and work it into the two

couplings. After it dries well, over an hour, hit it with water pressure. If there is a seep leak (unlikely), turn off the water, drain the system again and apply more glue to the leak.

If the burst pipe is copper, which is the most likely, the repair is again relatively simple. Drain the system and use a hacksaw to cut out the broken piece of pipe, going well back on both sides of the burst area to get completely free of the swelling.

Then get a propane torch, a small can of flux and a small roll of solder wire (the kind for plumbing). Along with these items buy a new piece of the right-diameter copper pipe, cut to fit in the place the old came out, and two slip-coupling tubes and a piece of fine emery paper.

First use the emery paper and sand the places where all the pipes will come together. Just abrade them enough to shine them up and clean them. When they are all sanded use the externals of the pipes and internals of the slip coupling tubes to "build" the repair section in place. Apply flux to each

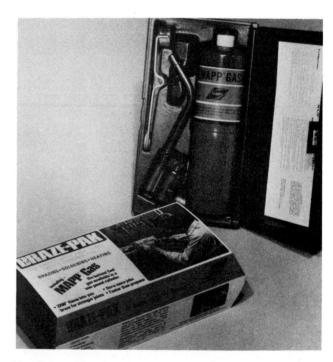

Heating and Brazing Outfit is made by Mapp Products. Gas cylinder with adjustable fuel regulator, hose length, torch and medium-duty high-velocity brazing tip (other tips available for special work).

joint as you put the pipe together, wiping well with the brush provided in the flux can. Do *no* soldering or heating at this time; just flux and build the whole repair in place.

When complete and in place use the propane torch as in the illustration, to "spray" heat the joints one at a time. Play the flame almost gently back and forth, holding the torch back three or four inches from the copper. Keep touching the joint area with the solder wire as you heat the copper. At a certain point you will note that the solder becomes melted by the copper—not by the torch, but by the copper. At the same moment it will "flow," actually seem to run of its own volition back into the seam between the coupling and the pipe. It is strange to see this happen; it

is almost like magic. Right then, when it runs or flows, run the wire end of the solder around the joint so a good load of solder goes back into the seam between the coupling and the pipe. Not a large amount—just a bit—and then back off by pulling the propane and solder away immediately. Allow it to cool, then do the same to the other end of the same coupling. Allow that to cool, then go to the other end of the pipe and repeat, one coupling seam at a time. Once the repair is finished and it has cooled for a while, turn the water on. There probably will not be a leak, but if there is you must turn everything off, redrain the system (any water left in the pipe will carry off the heat and not allow the copper to melt the solder) and repeat the soldering process at the leak area. Do not

Gently "spray" heat the joints one at a time, touching solder wire to joint area as you heat the pipe.

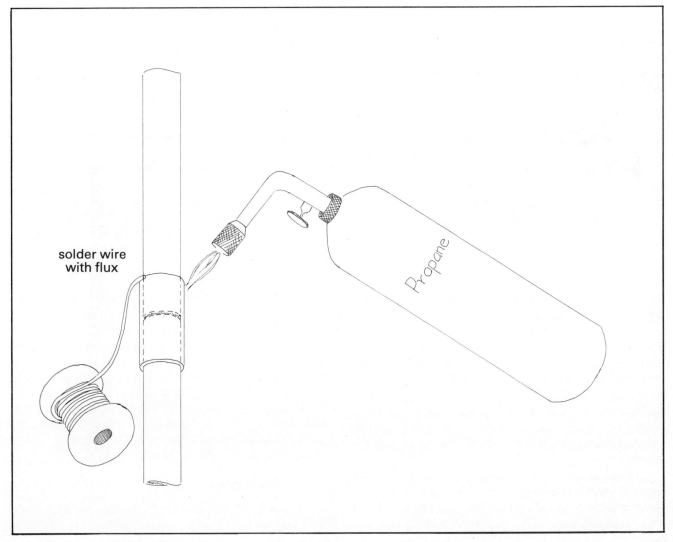

solder wire
with flux

overdo it, but heat the pipe until the solder runs, then back off. It should not take very much to fix the remaining leak.

A last note on copper-pipe leaks due to burst or frozen pipe: the most common area for this kind of problem is in a hot-water heating system. Usually this happens when the house is untended and the boiler goes out for one reason or another. And most often the break will occur *inside* one of the heating units, back in a low corner where the cold settles first.

The repair is the same as just described. The only difference is that the copper pipe is inside the heater housing on the baseboard. Take off the housing and then remove the radiation fins; the fins are easily taken off the break area. The copper pipe is cut out the same as in straight-pipe cases, and the couplings soldered in place. Then leave the fins off when done; they will not fit well once the couplings are soldered and may prevent heat distribution. This will not greatly impair the efficiency of the unit.

Hidden Problems. Catastrophic leaks that are hidden inside walls or ceilings require that the wall or ceiling be torn apart, the leak area exposed, the leak repaired; then the walls or ceiling is repaired as per methods explained in the appropriate chapter in this book.

Hot Water Heaters—Gas and Electric

The only thing that goes wrong with a hot water heater is that it lets the water get cold—gas heaters go out; electric heaters trip breakers.

For relighting gas heaters, follow the instructions on the little panel over the control opening that goes into the burner. They are usually very explicit, but it helps to hold the little button down—the safety button on the pilot light—until it seems your thumb will fall off. Go the full minute, and then some, or the burner will not stay on.

Electric hot water heaters will have a "reset" button somewhere. Find it, hold it in per instructions, and the heater will come back on. If not, and if the main breakers are not popped, the element might be burned out. These unscrew, pull straight out, and can be replaced by going to the appropriate dealer. Drop a new one in, screw the wires back on and hit the breaker *which you had turned off for safety before starting.*

Leaks around pipes coming out of hot water heaters should be repaired the same as regular pipe leaks (see section on pipe leaks). Just remember to let everything cool down in order to avoid burning

your hands, and drain the system back through the lowest drain. Also remember to turn the heating element, gas or electric, *off.*

Wells and Septic Systems

While not specifically having to do with plumbing, wells and septic systems fall into the same category and fit in best here.

Wells

With wells, and speaking from a strictly repair standpoint, there is relatively little that can be home repaired. Problems with wells tend to be major—polluted water, blown submerged pumps (by lightning), shifted and broken casings; none of the real problems with wells lend themselves to easy home repair. Often heavy equipment is needed to pull the well, or special purifying machinery is required. This type of work is beyond most homeowners.

Still, there are a few things that happen that can be "fixed" at home. First, a common mistake in working with wells is to overemphasize the problem. Do not jump to the expensive conclusion but check out the easy solution first. If the well suddenly stops, for instance, it does not necessarily mean the pump is blown. Check the power supply; make sure it is not just a breaker or fuse popped by a temporary overload condition, which is very common and usually the trouble. If everything seems normal, look for "hidden" safety systems. Quite often, as an example, there will be an overload breaker on the pressure tank or near the pressure switching system. Here again, a temporary surge or condition may have tripped the switch and caused the well to stop pumping. Be sure to reset all switches and replace all fuses before calling in outside help. If the breaker pops repeatedly, or fuses keep blowing, then the problem is more complicated and will require knowledgeable help.

Under absolutely *no* condition should you take chances with your health and your water supply. If you even slightly suspect that the water has gone bad or changed; if there is just a faint new odor or strange taste; stop drinking the water at once. Take a sample to the county health board and get it analyzed. It will not take long and costs little or nothing. Some pretty terrible things come from polluted water, some of them crippling and fatal. Don't chance it.

Septic Systems

If a septic system is put in properly and a tile field well laid out and installed, there is very little that

know your water heater

Cut away view of a typical gas-fired water heater (on right) and an electric hot water heater (at left). These units are relatively simple and you should get to know yours. Control unit in gas heater is at lower left and in electric heater it is found beneath plates on top and bottom of the tank. You should use these control units; you can turn your heater to lowest setting for general use (120°) or switch the entire unit off when you are away from home for several days (A. O. Smith Co.).

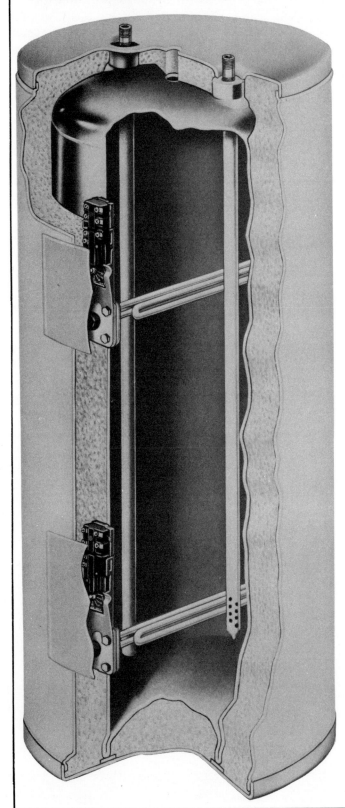
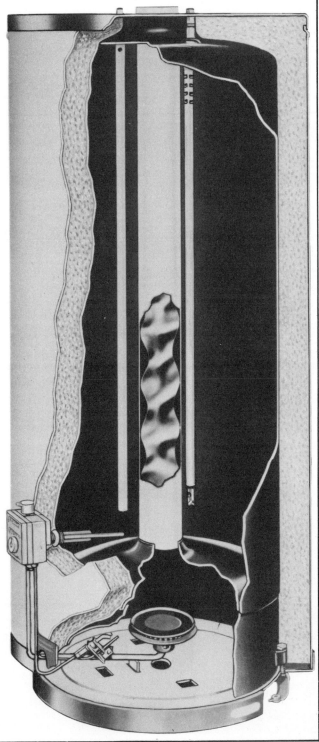

can go wrong. With normal usage, and a moderate approach to water-dumping appliances like dishwashers, a good septic system will last virtually forever.

When they go bad it usually is because the system was not made right in the first place, and the symptom is inevitably that the tank and/or tile field overflows and allows raw sewage (with attendant mess and smells) to come out on the lawn. Or the basement drain backs up and does not respond to treatment with a plumbing snake.

Proper repair involves redigging and relaying the field, after probably blasting it with dynamite to "loosen" the base rock and soil. It is as complicated, difficult and dangerous as it sounds.

If it is necessary to tear the septic out or the yard is damaged, you will find that new grass really *does* grow wildly over the septic. Just rake and reseed and *do not* fertilize. If you have to fill with dirt and are wondering how to quickly calculate the amount of dirt to order in cubic yards, just remember that a space three feet by three feet on the sides and one foot deep equals a third of a "yard" (a cubic yard is 27 cubic feet). Somehow it is not as hard to visualize a third—three-by-three by one foot thick—of a cubic yard whereas a whole one is hard to measure in your mind. Any extra, hold and use to fill in as the new soil compacts. Order about ten percent extra to be safe.

It is possible, however, to effect at least a temporary kind of "repair" without going through the insanity of getting in heavy equipment and tearing the yard apart.

If your septic system begins to come out the top, vastly curtail the use of your drain system for a couple of weeks. Stop using the dishwasher, likewise the clothes washer (go to the laundromat), and cut down on the number of showers. No baths; they use too much water. What you're doing is cutting down the intake completely to the tank and tile field and allowing the ground to dry out; quite literally giving the earth a rest.

Very often this rest and rejuvenation period will be enough to allow the system to come back to normal. You still will not be able to run amok and use the dishwasher every hour, but if you hold back for a couple of weeks it will let the ground back off the saturation point enough to make the system at least usable.

If just backing off does not "repair" the septic system, the problems are more severe. A spring may have started feeding into the tile field or a pipe may have burst—and there is no home remedy that will work.

Note. Sometimes septics quit "working"; that is the tank no longer functions in a bacterial sense and does not work the solids down to a liquid that the tile field can handle. This might be noted by the system backing up, but more often it will be a smell that *cannot* be ignored.

Toilet Repairs

Chipped Enamel

Use a liquid procelain glaze patching compound for chips. Badly cracked toilet fixtures cannot be repaired and should be replaced.

Fiberglass Surfaces

Never use scouring powders or pads on a fiberglass surface. Minor stains and cigarette burns can be removed by rubbing *lightly* with 600 grit sandpaper and a small amount of scouring powder. Repolish with automotive wax.

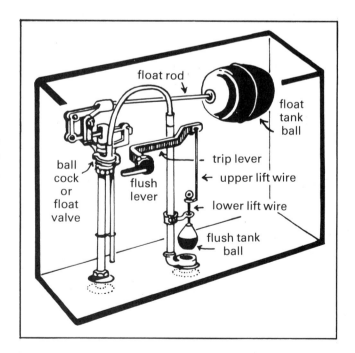

Schematic of toilet tank

Mechanical Problems

Leaks, Squeaks, and Whistles. The cause may be that the water supply does not shut off or the outlet valve does not close—or both. Mechanisms within the water tanks vary but are designed to produce enough water for thorough flushing, and replacement within a minute or so. The accompanying sketch of the most common mechanism found within a water closet shows what should happen when you push the handle to flush the toilet. The rod attached to the handle lifts the tank ball, opens the outlet, and permits water to flow into the toilet bowl. The tank ball then falls back into place, closing the outlet; the tank is refilled from the inlet tube. As the water refills the tank it raises the float ball, which measures the water and closes the supply valve at the proper level.

If water continues to run into the bowl, some part of the mechanism is out of order. Leaks are usually caused by improper seating of the tank ball. Check to see that the ball wire and rod guide are not bent. Or there could be a worn washer in the intake valve. To replace this washer you will have to remove a lever; remember to shut off the water supply to the tank before beginning.

The "Plumber's Helper." This is usually the first attempt in fixing a clogged toilet. However, instead of the bulb-type suction-cup style used for sinks, you

how to repair a toilet

Leaky flush valves attributable to conventional toilet tank mechanism can be eliminated with a Flusher Fixer Kit available from hardware and lumber dealers. The kit replaces the worn-out tank ball or flapper and does away with lift wires and brackets that often become bent. Unlike conventional flush valve assemblies, the Flusher Fixer Kit is installed without tools and without removing the tank from the bowl. The kit's seat is simply bonded directly onto the existing seat with a patented watertight sealant.

As detailed in the accompanying photographs, on page 68, the old tank stopper ball is first removed from the toilet along with the left wires and bracket guide. (1) Steel wool is then used to clean off the old brass flush valve seat and water used to rinse the seat clean. (2) Waterproof sealant is applied to the underside of the new stainless steel ring using the entire contents of the tube supplied with the kit (Illustration 3).

After placement of the new seat on the old brass seat, a 9-ounce can is placed atop the unit (3) to apply necessary bonding weight. The seat is allowed to set in this position for two hours with water level just enough to cover the top rim of the seat. A chain is then secured to the flush valve (4) and attached to the lift arm. Excess chain may be cut off or fastened to the clip and the toilet is ready to use.

need a molded-force-ball type; it exerts a lot more pressure. Leave several inches of water in the toilet bowl and insert the plunger into the opening. Start pumping. If the plunger does not handle the repair, you may need a closet auger to break loose the obstruction. If this does not work, the toilet will have to be removed from the floor.

Installing Toilet Tank and Bowl

The first requirement is a thoroughly clean floor surface where the toilet will be located. Then follow these steps or the instructions supplied by the manufacturer.

A. Place the fixture upside down on a protective soft material to prevent scratching, and apply a warmed wax ring to the circular recess at the base of the bowl. The fixture will be connected to the waste line through this recess. Then apply a setting compound to the outer rim of the bowl to assure a continuous seal to the floor.

B. Set the bowl carefully atop the metal flange already attached on the floor. The toilet bolts fit through the holes in the base of the fixture, ready to receive washers and nuts. Tighten these snugly, but do not force-tighten or you will strip the threads.

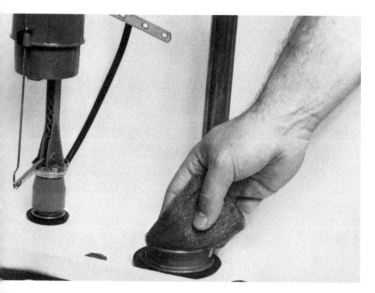

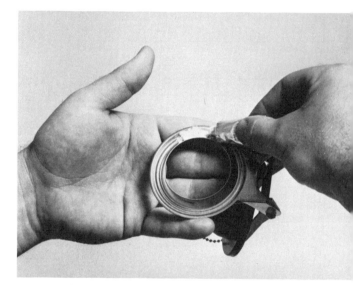

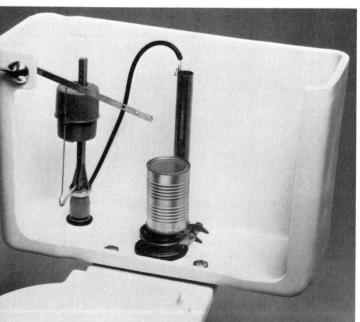

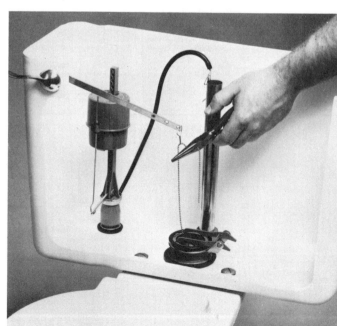

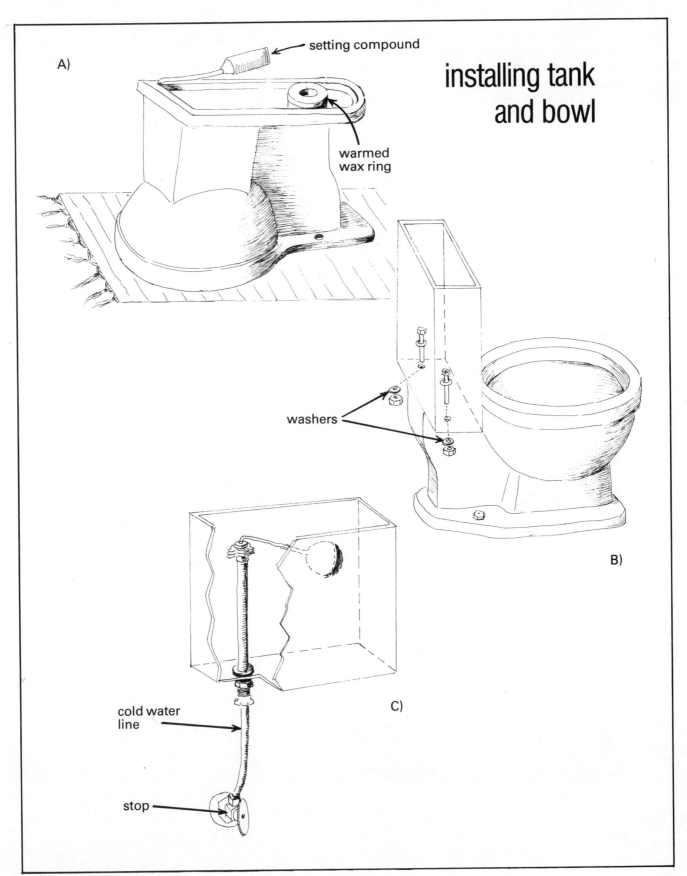

A) setting compound

warmed wax ring

installing tank and bowl

B)

washers

C)

cold water line

stop

Following placement of large donut-shaped washers on the threaded tank outlet, place the tank on the ledge of the bowl and align for placement of bolts downward through the bolt holes of the two parts. Again, the bolts should be tightened carefully, alternating from side to side to prevent breaking the tank or bowl.

C. The cold-water line must then be connected to the tank with a straight or angle stop. Now you can insert the ballcock into the tank and secure it in position. This mechanism varies according to the unit purchased, so read installation instructions on the package.

Turn water on by opening the angle or straight stop located beneath the tank. The tank should fill to the "water line" indicated inside the tank. If it does not, the brass rod supporting the ball float should be bent until the tank stops filling at the water line.

chapter nine

electrical problems

There are two very important facts to remember when considering electrical problems, two points so vital that they must be stressed at the outset.

First, at some point in dealing with household electrical difficulties—at some critical juncture in repairing home electrical problems—the work becomes a life-threatening job. This is true for anybody; 110 volts (out of the outlet power) can easily be fatal to even a young, healthy person. For somebody with heart problems it is doubly so; even the slightest shock can then be fatal and *extreme* caution should be used at all times.

- Never touch a wire you suspect might be hot.
- Never put anything but the accepted type of plug into an outlet.
- Never bypass safety equipment like fuses or appliance interlocks.
- Never hurry.
- Never work beyond your knowledge; if you do not know what you are doing, stop.
- Never take *any* chances—do not for instance, even touch a power tool if you are standing in water.

The second thing you must remember about electricity is that—with the exception of lightning—there are no "surprises" in electrical problems. If a fuse blows or a circuit breaker pops, it is most definitely because something caused an overload on the line. And if you replace the fuse or reset the breaker and it happens again, you have a problem that can-

ELECTRICAL TROUBLE-SHOOTING CHART
BASIC PROBLEMS

Symptoms	Breakers, fuses in main box	Power outage, call elec. co.	Calling to check on excess power (surge on the line)	Checking for plug and cord	Checking device in different outlets	Checking for bad appliance or tool (cut power to room with odor)
All lights and power out	X	X				
Lights out to one room	X					
Dim lights (low or slow operation of appliances)		X				
Persistently blowing fuse or popping breaker			X		X	X
High power bills						
Burnt smell in air						X
Warm feeling on wall near outlet						X
Inoperative appliance or tool, TV or stereo				X	X	
Flickering or blinking lights		X				
Turn to repair info. on . . .						

home appliance wattage

Appliance	Wattage	Appliance	Wattage
air conditioning**	window unit 9000 Btu/hr	freezer (15 cu. ft.)	manual defrost 341 watts
	central system 24,000 Btu/hr		frost-free 440 watts
baby food warmer	165 watts	fry pan*	1200 watts
blanket*	150 watts	garage door opener	(⅓ hp)
blender	385 watts	griddle*	1200 watts
broiler (portable)	1140 watts	hair dryers	soft bonnet 400 watts
can opener	100 watts		hard bonnet 900 watts
carving knife	95 watts		hand held 600 watts
clock	2.5 watts		
clothes dryer	4900 watts		
clothes washer (automatic)	512 watts	hair setter/curler	350 watts
coffee maker	600 watts	heating pad*	60 watts
corn popper	575 watts	humidifier	177 watts
curling iron	40 watts	ice cream freezer	130 watts
deep fat fryer*	1200 watts	ice crusher	100 watts
dehumidifier	257 watts	iron*	1100 watts
dishwasher	1200 watts	juicer	90 watts
disposer	445 watts	knife sharpener	40 watts
electronic cleaner	50 watts	lighting	
electric heating**		make-up mirror	20 watts
egg cooker	550 watts	microwave oven	1450 watts
fans	window 200 watts	mixer	hand 80 watts
	furnace or central air 270 watts		stand 150 watts
floor polisher	305 watts		
fondue/chafing dish*	800 watts	radio	25 watts

You can use these wattage amounts to calculate the load on a line, and judge whether or not an overload has resulted in a loss of power.

Appliance	Wattage	Appliance	Wattage
range	12,200 watts	vacuum cleaner	650 watts
	self-cleaning process*	waffle iron*	1200 watts
		warming tray	140 watts
roaster*	1425 watts	water heater	general use
refrigeragor (12 cu. ft.)	manual defrost 241 watts		for clothes washer
	frost-free 321 watts	water pump	1000 watts
refrigerator/freezer (14 cu. ft.)	manual defrost 326 watts	workshop and hobby equipment	
	frost-free 615 watts		
sewing machine	75 watts		
shaver	15 watts		
shaving cream dispenser	60 watts		
slow cooker	200 watts		
stereo/hi-fi	109 watts		
sun lamp	290 watts		
television	black & white, tube-type 160 watts		
	black & white, solid state 55 watts		
	color, tube-type 300 watts		
	color, solid state 200 watts		
toaster	1400 watts		
toothbrush	1.1 watts		
trash compactor	400 watts		

*Thermostatically controlled. Cost based on appliance estimated "On" time.

**Electric heating and air conditioning costs vary with each home. Many items affect an accurate estimate: size of home, type of system, amount of insulation, number of doors, windows, etc. On the above chart, kwh usage estimated for air conditioning represents an average for central Indiana for each of four cooling months. Kwh usage in northern Indiana would be lower; usage in southern Indiana would be higher. For information on your electric heating or cooling costs, call the nearest Public Service office.

Electrical service entrance may be overhead or underground. Shown here is a typical entrance enclosure with meter base for an underground service drop. At right, meter and enclosure cover in place once home has been completed.

not be wished away. This will take on more importance as you get into specific repair methods.

For some reason people insist that there are weird "temporary" difficulties that appear and then disappear in electrical systems. Or they do not believe the external indications they see; they continue to ignore popped fuses and breakers and try to work around them.

As for specific problems and repairs, they are covered below in order of frequency.

Overload—popped breaker or fuse

This situation is the most common electrical problem for the homeowner. It means that something on the line, something in the home, has demanded more power than the system is capable of furnishing safely. In the case of a circuit breaker, a heat-sensing switch has opened and killed the power supply; in the case of a blown fuse a thin strip of metal has melted (literally) and broken the circuit. In either case, the power is cut off and the actual cause (at this point) could be almost anything.

For that reason the best repair method might be called the ever-more-complicated approach. Start with the simplest possible cause—a surge in current popped the breaker—a temporary line surge. This is rarely the case, however, since electrical power is usually more reliable than that. Still, it is worth checking out.

Always try resetting the breaker first. Wait a few moments until it has cooled, then reset or replace the fuse. If that works, you have achieved the simplest repair possible.

If it does not work, widen your scope of inquiry and go the the next-most-complicated possible cause. Remember, something *made* the breaker pop, and that problem began recently. It also would help if you went around the room or area without power, and listed the appliances that were plugged in at the time. Then add up the watts (if not visibly marked, use the chart provided here for an estimate) and you may have your answer without further ado. Most lines will not service more than 2200 watts. Or consider whether you have recently plugged in a light or an appliance on the line. Whatever the size, this recent additional load could be causing the overload. Unplug it, try resetting again, and see whether or not the overload has disappeared.

If you are still faced with loss of power, advance to the next-most-difficult-to-verify possibility: Has some piece of older equipment on the line—a light or appliance—suddenly gone bad?

Begin repair by unplugging appliances controlled by that breaker or fuse; take everything external off the line. When it is clear except for built-in lights, hit the breaker again. It will probably hold this time because appliances are generally the cause of popped fuses or breakers. Then simply plug them back in one at a time until the culprit pops the breaker. You may be able to choose which appliance should be removed from the line. For example, anything portable may be moved to another line with less demand on it.

If taking all appliances off the line still does not answer your problem, widen the scope once again. Have you, or somebody else, done something recently that might cause the breaker to snap? A new nail accidentally driven into a wire would do it, or a mower cutting through an outside wire....there is a physical cause for that popping breaker.

At this point you have reached the juncture where you are involved with life-threatening forces. It is at this stage—and in all fairness it is best to point out that by this time in looking for the problem virtually all simple home difficulties should be solved—that exposure to electricity becomes necessary. Up to now it has simply been a matter of plugging and unplugging things.

If the breakers still pop, it is necessary to begin removing outlets and light fixtures on the rare possibility that something inside one of them is causing the sudden difficulty.

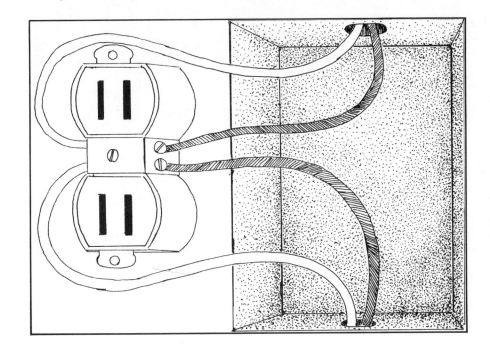

The "guts" of an outlet pulled out, black wires on one side, white on the other. Outlets are not complicated, but be cautious. Remember to always work with power off.

Caution is the most important element while carrying out this final attempt to solve the problem. Be absolutely positive that all power is *off* to the house. When you have verified it yourself, then use a screwdriver and remove the cover plate on the first outlet on the circuit that keeps blowing.

With the cover plate off, visually examine the outlet inside. Make certain there are no burned spots, no blown-black carbon areas, assuming it is all clean and clear, do the same with every outlet on the line. Remove all the cover plates and leave them off. Then visually go over them without touching anything to see if you can find some evidence of trouble.

You probably will. Electricity often leaves traces when it gets out of hand. But if you cannot see anything obviously wrong, begin to take the covers off the light fixtures in the ceiling—just remove the screws and drop all the external covers to check for damage.

If you find either a burnt outlet or light fixture—and keep the power off—remove the outlet or fixture and put a new one in *exactly* the way the old one came out. Put the new black wire where it came off the old one, the new white wire back on the new one exactly as it came off the old, and the new green or bare wire to ground—all just the same. Working with wiring scares some people, but taking out things and putting in the new is really quite simple and basic. Just follow the old pattern exactly; if you have any doubt, draw a quick sketch before you remove the old

wiring. All wiring is color-coded—black is power, white neutral, and green or bare wire is the common ground. Draw a small picture showing what colored wires go where, and that will be all you need to know. Nothing is complicated; just do not hurry, and work within your knowledge. If you do something wrong, the worst that should happen is that the breaker will pop when you resupply the power.

A last thought on working this way, in ever-expanding circles: the chances of ever getting to the point of pulling outlets or light fixtures is minimal. This discussion is for methodology, but in virtually all cases the trouble will show itself right away, and will turn out to be something plugged in or new to the line.

Nonworking Power—No Juice

The second most common electrical problem is lack of power when you plug in an appliance or tool.

Again, the search for the root of the trouble, and method for effecting repair, requires working in expanding circles.

The probable cause is a faulty tool or appliance. Quickly grab another tool and plug it into the same outlet to verify whether or not the tool actually works. If the new tool works where the old one did not, then either repair the tool or take it back to the manufac-

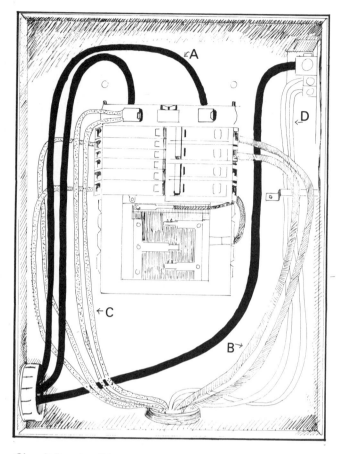

Circuit Breaker Diagram:
A—Input from power lines, coming in through transformer;
B—circuit wire throughout house;
C—220 volts to range and appliances;
D—neutral, ground wires.

1. Unscrew screws holding old switch box.

2. Remove old wires from switch.

3. Rewire in new switch.

turer; actually, in all cases take it back to the manufacturer. There are far too many substandard tools being built.

In almost all cases the tool or appliance will be the problem rather than the power source. But for purposes of repair methods, let us assume that the tool or appliance is not faulty; the second try does not work either.

Expand the scope of repair work. Go back to the breaker or fuse box and verify that a breaker or fuse has not popped. Working with pure probability, usually loss of power is due to a breaker or fuse. Reset and if it does not hold, work it out as an overload problem (just discussed).

If a rare occasion has come up and the tool is good, and the breaker has not popped, verify that the house as a whole has power. Make certain that there

4. *Replace in box.*

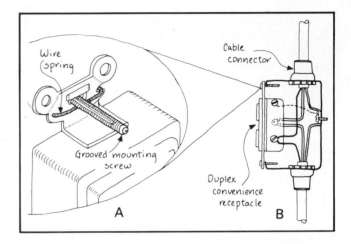

Receptacle grounding detail indicates two methods of providing adequate electrical bonding of the switch or outlet receptacle to the electrical box to maintain grounding continuity. In sketch (A), a built-in wire spring is provided in some devices so proper box contact is made when the device is screwed to the box. In sketch (B), an alternative method. The dashed line which represents a bonding jumper wire from the bonding screw terminal to the box ground screw. The National Electrical Code requires bonding of all electrical system enclosures such as raceways, cable armor, cable sheath, frames, fittings and other noncurrent-carrying metal parts.

5. *Add new cover plate.*

is electrical power coming in by checking a light or two. Sometimes a power outage will hit during the day and there will be no ready indication, so check around.

If power is available to the house, but still is not going through to the outlets even though you know the breaker is reset, the problem approaches that point where it is perhaps best to call the electrician. Something has caused the wire to open suddenly: the insulation wrapping may be torn, or the wire has been cut or melted itself apart. The repair can be dangerous from the standpoint of the fire precaution and leaking current. When safety becomes a critical issue, it is best to call in outside help.

Non-Grounded Circuits or Appliances

Now and then you will experience a tingling sensation when you touch the sink and an appliance at the same time—a mild shock. This is caused by imperfect grounding of the appliance through the circuits, usually in older homes where there is no ground circuit.

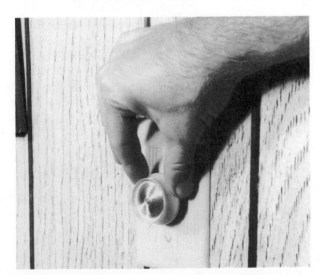

6. *And press switch knob in place over spindle.*

The repair is to use a wire from some metal part of the cover or case—a sheetmetal screw on the back works well—to the nearest proper ground. Just run the wire from a screw to a ground clamp (purchased from the nearest hardware) on a waterpipe, either supply or drain. The ground clamp is cheap and easily installed; you can use any spare electrical wire you can find to do the job. If you haven't any wire, a single strand of 16 gauge wire will do nicely. Strip insulating material from the ends; one end clamps to the appliance and the other to the water pipe.

Ground fault interrupter is combined with a duplex convenience outlet in this Leviton-made device, which should be used for outdoor outlets and in other hazardous locations where the entire circuit is not protected by a GFI-type breaker at the circuit distribution panel. The interrupter is sensitive to leaking current protecting against the possibility of serious shocks. It includes a test button to verify that the mechanism is operating.

Appliance Problems

In all truth several lifetimes could be spent and many books written just on appliance problems. One washer or refrigerator is so complicated that discussing complete repair would take weeks. Still, there are ways to avoid paying a great deal of money for very little work.

The main thing with appliance repair is to verify that you actually have a problem before you call the repairman or take it into the shop. Many—most—times a small, temporary thing will cause indications of a major difficulty and unscrupulous repairmen will charge more than the job is worth. When the appliance begins to malfunction, or when it stops, evaluate what is happening carefully before getting help.

First, did the plug come loose from the wall? It sounds ridiculous, but many people still pay for so-called "repairs" when appliances have simply come unplugged. So, check the plug.

Second, and this is especially true of washers and dryers, look to see that the reset button (wherever it is hidden) has not been tripped. Most larger appliances have their own circuit breakers, called "reset buttons," somewhere in the back or underneath. A temporary load condition (i.e., too many clothes in a dryer) can trip this breaker.

First the plug, then the reset button. If they are both working properly, go back and check the circuit breaker or fuse in the house circuitry.

Assume for as long as possible that the appliance is actually all right and that there is something else causing the problem.

Finally, when you are certain it isn't merely a circuit breaker or the plug has not come loose from the wall, check where the power line is connected to the appliance. Often moving an appliance will work the cord loose and you might find it simply a matter of tightening a screw or replugging a loose plug.

In the end, if the appliance is bad, try the manufacturer before you call the repairman. Even if the appliance is old, even if you do not think it is a defect, drop a note to them and explain that it broke down and ask them to fix it. It will surprise you how often they actually will either fix it or at least absorb part of the cost of labor and/or material.

chapter ten
heating systems

Repair of heating systems varies dramatically with the type of system, type of energy source, type of control method, and type of installation in individual application.

Types of Systems

Brief descriptions are given here for heating systems available which conform to generalized repair methods.

TROUBLESHOOTING CHART
HEATING SYSTEMS

Symptoms	Thermostat (wires soldered in thermostat?)	Lack of energy source	Heater breaker check	Main house breaker check	Change filters	Dust on	Lint in grates	Calling about general power outage	Opening in duct to room	Jammed duct stop (grate cover)	Obstruction of grate (box or drape)	Oil blower bearing	Oil pump bearing	Fitting on heater element or radiator
No heat to house	X	X	X	X				X						
No heat to room	X		X				X		X	X	X			
Low heat to house	X	X			X	X	X	X				X		
Low heat to room	X				X	X	X		X	X	X			
Strange "labored" sound from heating system					X			X				X	X	
Dampness on wall/floor														X
Slight chill; shoulder chill	X				X	X	X	X	X	X				
Dust from forced air duct					X				X					
Noticeable high humidity														X
Breaker won't hold on blower motor					X			X				X		
High-pitched squeal from heating system					X							X	X	

Turn to repair info on . . .

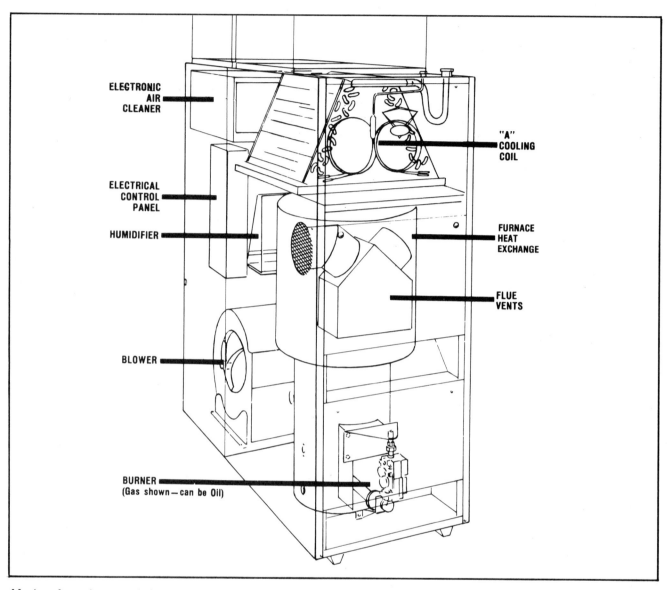

ELECTRONIC AIR CLEANER

"A" COOLING COIL

ELECTRICAL CONTROL PANEL

HUMIDIFIER

FURNACE HEAT EXCHANGE

FLUE VENTS

BLOWER

BURNER (Gas shown—can be Oil)

Modern forced warm-air furnaces are very popular; this one heats with gas (Dept. of Agriculture).

Forced Air Systems

The most common system: air is heated—usually in a flame chamber or by electrical methods—and then blown through ducting throughout the house.

Hot Water Heating

Second most common, in the system the water is heated and run through the house in piping, with a radiator unit in each room.

Electrical Baseboard Heating

In each room an electrical heating unit along the baseboard—usually a straight radiator with hot wires or a water filled unit heated by electrical wires—is controlled by a thermostat.

Radiation Ceiling Units

Electrical wires *in* the drywall in the ceiling—actually embedded in the material—are made warm by current. The wires radiate heat down into the room.

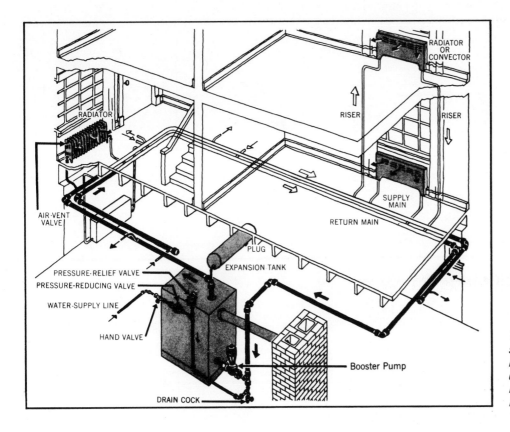

Two-pipe forced hot-water system has one pipe supplying hot water to the room-heating units while the other pipe returns cooled water to the boiler (Dept. of Agriculture).

Steam Radiation Units

A boiler in the basement heats steam and the steam is circulated through the house through piping, with radiators in each room; very old houses use this method, which is usually cranky.

Maintenance

As might be expected, and as covered briefly in the first chapter, the best method of heating system "repair" is a good maintenance system. Keep it clean and running right and you probably won't have to worry about specific repairs.

To that end, listed below are some maintenance considerations which can help a great deal (they will be followed by specific repair procedures for breakdown situations).

Electric heating cable is usually located in the ceiling. (Dept. of Agriculture)

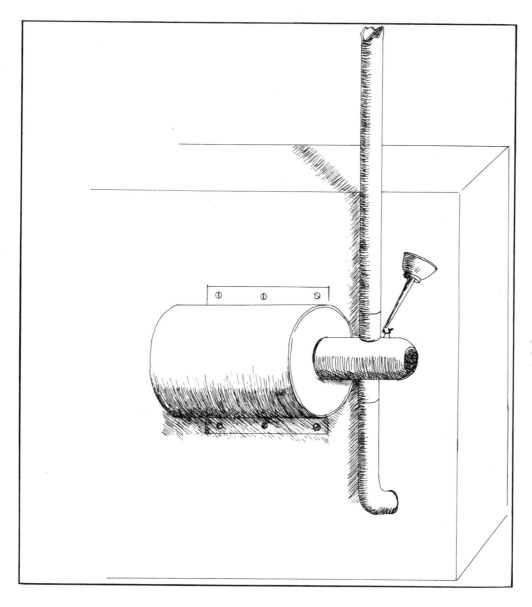

All you need are two or three squirts of oil into the bearings on the pump motor.

Keep the filters fresh. This is for forced air systems, obviously, but clean filters allow a much easier air flow and more heat for less money.

Actual replacement of filters is simply a matter of removing the access panel on the side of the heater —it is clearly marked—and sliding the air filter out. Just throw it away and replace it with one of the correct size.

Keep the floor grates clean of lint—use the vacuum cleaner to insure easy movement of air.

Wrap the heater ducts in the basement with insulation; just wrap and tape if they are exposed. The heat loss from bare ducts is enormous.

Make sure all joints in ducting are taped with duct tape and are airtight. (While doing this you might check around basement windows and use the tape to make a tight air seal and to keep cold air from being "sucked" into the basement by the heater system.)

Oil the bearings on the blower fan. Or, if you have a hot water heating system, oil the bearings on the pump motor. Pump bearings are inside the pump motor on the hot water heating system (on the side of the boiler assembly). On the motor there will be a small oil-cap filler area. Lift the little spring-lid device and squirt a touch of oil in the hole.

For hot water systems, use a vacuum cleaner to take all dust off all the baseboard units. Take the covers off and vacuum down in the pipes and fins. Dust greatly affects the heat-transfer qualities of the fin system.

Check the entire hot water system for seep-leaks,

especially on the hot water side of the piping, where it goes up to the actual heating elements. Leaks can be fixed by draining the system and soldering as previously covered, but if allowed to continue they will lose more heat than you think. Drops add up fast.

Soap-check all exposed gas connections, whether you have a hot water system or forced air. Use soap bubbles to check all joints to make sure there are no leaks. (Gas leaks will make obvious bubbles in the soap.) To repair, tighten the fitting with a wrench.

Vacuum the outside of the heater—again, whether it is forced air or hot water. Dust will get into bearings, blowers, fittings and flame jets. If kept clean, there will be less trouble down the line.

Specific-Trouble Repairs

As previously stated, there are so many different kinds of systems that going into detail on any one

Cutaway of an oil-fired boiler, available with completely enclosed jacket (Dept. of Agriculture).

could take volumes. There are, however, basic repair methods that apply to all.

As with many other forms of household repairs, the most dangerous thing you can do is to jump to expensive conclusions. Then, too, there are so many shady operators dealing in the whole area of heating systems that it is best to exhaust all possibilities before calling the contractor. Do not assume anything, and only call in professional help when you're absolutely sure you cannot fix it yourself. The truth is that most heating systems are very simple and well-made, and genuinely break down only rarely.

If the heat just stops, which is the most common trouble symptom, don't reach for the phone. First go down in the basement or wherever the heater is located and visually study it. Don't just look at it, but listen to it as well.

Most often the energy supply has stopped. If you have a gas input, check to make certain the gas is still coming to the heater, and that there is flame in the flame compartment. If you are on electricity, ascertain that the breakers have not popped and cut off the energy. Really get in there and look.

If there is flame or heat energy evident, check the

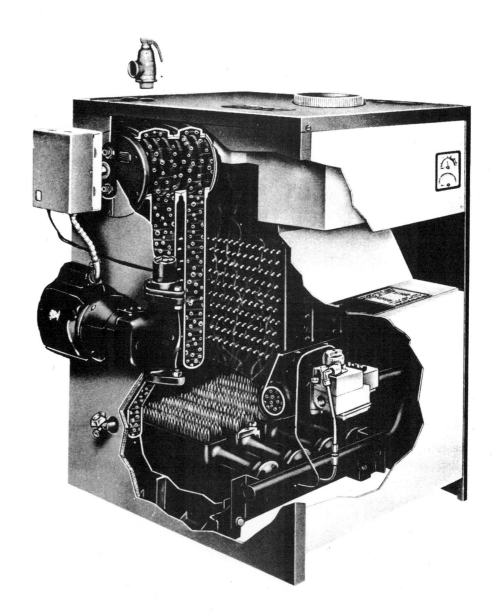

Cutaway of a gas boiler, showing components.

The Anatomy of a Fireplace

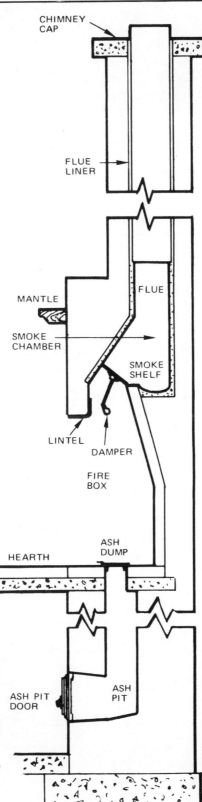

Chimney Cap
Available precast for some standard flue sizes or cast in place. Note that the liner projects through the cap several inches.

Smoke Chamber
Together with the smoke shelf, this area is important to a smoke free fire. Both sides slope to the flue and it is important that they slope identically, otherwise the fire will burn on one side of the firebox only.

The entire smoke chamber and smoke shelf is parged with fire clay mortar (refractory mortar) or type "S" mortar one-half inch thick.

Throat and Damper
These parts are usually one and the same. The damper is capable of being opened and closed gradually to control the draft and keep out cold air when the fireplace is not in use. The opening in square inches should be at least 90% of that required for the flue.

Firebox
This is the area that comes alive with dancing flames and gleaming embers. To do this the firebox must be correctly proportioned, sealed, vented, and well constructed.

Hearth
The inner hearth is that portion within the fire area and is usually built of fire brick but may be other types of hard brick, concrete, stone, tile or other non-combustible heat-resistant materials. The outer hearth is built of the same type materials and should extend a minimum of eight inches on each side of the fireplace opening and sixteen inches in front. (Note: These figures are twelve inches and eighteen inches in areas covered by the Uniform Building Code.)

Flue and Flue Lining
The area of the flue should equal one-twelfth to one-eighth the area of the opening of the fireplace (width times height). Lining is supported on masonry.

Smoke Shelf
This is a horizontal shelf, usually concave and extending backward from the rear of the throat or damper to the rear flue wall. It directs cold air downdrafts which are present in the early stages of the fire, causing them to eddy and drift upward with the rising air currents.

Ashpit
This is the hollow space below the hearth into which ashes fall through the ash dump door located in the hearth. A metal door is provided in the ashpit for the occasional removal of ashes. In basementless homes, particularly those built on a concrete slab, it may not be feasible to provide an ashpit unless the hearth has been raised. In this case the ashpit door faces outside.

Foundation
Consult your local building code, since these codes differ according to existing soil and moisture conditions in individual areas. If total weight is needed to compute the depth and rise of the foundation required, figure brick at 130 lbs. and concrete at 150 lbs. per cubic foot. For cubic footage, figure the entire cross section volume including the open portion of the flue and firebox. The footing should extend at least below the depth of the greatest frost penetration.

As a general rule, footings should be of concrete at least twelve inches thick and should extend at least six inches on all sides of the foundation. Concrete should be poured on undisturbed soil.

Foundation walls should be a minimum of eight inches thick.

distribution system. It could be that a blower or pump has tripped a "reset" switch—quite common. If so, reset the switch by pushing it in and holding it for a moment and then wait to see if everything kicks on and works properly. Line surge or temporary over load could trigger the breaker (which might be more sensitive than the regular house breakers) and the trouble may not occur again for years.

If there is flame or heat energy, and no breaker is tripped, check back at the regular house breakers. If they have not been tripped (again quite common), then the trouble may be approaching a point where it is necessary to call in a contractor.

The main thing is to approach the system with logic. When there is no heat to the house, look to the source of the heat. If there is fire or energy in the flame chamber, check the distribution. If there is no evident problem there (a visually burned-out motor, a switch knocked accidentally off), then recheck.

Relighting Pilot Lights (gas or propane)

First and most important, find the written instructions on the heater in the vicinity of the pilot. Keep looking until you find them—they are somewhere near. If there are no instructions, a general method follows:

(1) turn the gas control knob to the "pilot" position;

(2) light a match or twisted piece of paper and hold it at the little nozzle where the pilot light burns (easily seen);

(3) depress the pilot light "push-button" near the gas control knob and note that pilot light ignites—hold button down for a full minute, then more, until pilot light stays ignited when push-button is released;

(4) turn gas control knob to "on" or "heat" position and note that heater comes on.

Only call in a heating contractor when you have completely exhausted your own abilities to study the systems involved. And then do so only with utmost caution, and watch the repairman while he works on the heater.

A final thought on heating systems: if you are in a fairly new home (ten or so years or less) check for a home manual for the type of heating system. If there is one available, read it from page one. If you are just buying a home, it is a good idea to get addresses from equipment tags on various and sundry appliances and write away for the manual for each item. It can mean a difference of hundreds of dollars,

Handicap of Too Large a Fireplace. Top—fireplace too large for fire. Radiates less heat than where flame fits the fireplace smoothly—as bottom.

literally, in future home repair bills. Many of the manuals even include problem-solving breakdown charts which greatly simplify repair work and practically nullify the need for calling in a contractor.

Fireplaces

Smoke Backup

When a chimney fails to draw properly for no known obvious reason, it does not necessarily mean you have a serious problem. Usually the reason for a smoke backup situation is that the chimney is cold and is sending cold air falling back down, carrying smoke with it.

First, get some ventilation in the room so there's no chance of suffocation.

Twist a newspaper, light the end and, before lighting a normal fire in the fireplace or heating unit, allow the flames from the newspaper to go up the chimney, establishing an upward movement of hot air.

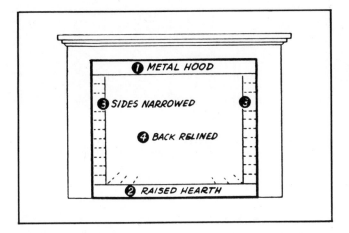

The flue area should not be less than the area of the fire-place opening. Where too small to carry off products of combustion, remedy may be found in reducing the size of the opening. Some corrective measures (1) install a shallow hood of metal beneath the fireplace breast. This also helps in cases where the damper position is too low. (2) Other ways of reducing the opening are to raise the hearth by laying one or two courses of brick over the old hearth. (3) Where drastic reduction is needed narrow the sides of the opening.

This will almost always stop smoke backup. If not, call a chimney-cleaning company to unclog the flue.

Method of Sealing Joints

A method of closing uncemented flue joints without tearing out the chimney has been used with success in some instances. It involves the use of a traveling plug and fairly thin grout. As a plug, a canvas bag is sometimes employed, stuffed with rags or papers and weighted with bricks in the bottom. When lowered into a flue from the top, by means of a line or pole, it should fit fairly tight, but not too tight for motion. The method of use is to stop it just below the level of each flue joint and pour grout down the flue. When stopped by the plug, the grout flows into the open joint. After the joint appears filled, the plug may be lifted and lowered a few times, producing a swabbing effect. Then it is lowered to the succeeding joint and the operation repeated.

Ashpit Clogged

Difficulty sometimes encountered in removing ashes from ashpits may be handled by making pits

This operation should be carried out with careful eye to conditions in the fireplace below. If too much grout is passing the plug, it may pile up on the smoke shelf, drain into the fireplace and deface it, or, in hardening, may impair the working of the damper.

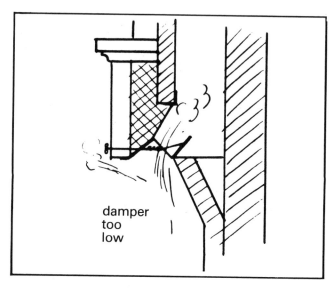

with uniform sectional areas and smoothing walls. When pits or chutes are offset in passing a fireplace on a lower floor, all possible care must be taken to avoid roughness or sharp changes of direction. Wall leakage, particularly in the basement wall, permits water to seep in and convert ashes into a soaked and tightly packed mass. More difficult conditions may call for tearing out masonry and treating obstructions.

Smokiness often ensues because the damper has been installed with its front flange at the lower level of the front wall, serving as a support for the brickwork. The remedy is to lower the top of the opening by adding one or two courses of brick, resting on an angle lintel.

chapter eleven
paints and finishes

Broadly speaking, dealing with paints and finishes becomes a matter of bracketing the finishes in categories.

Either it is an exterior covering or an interior one; either it is a water base or an oil base finish; either it is enamel- or latex(acrylic)-based paint.

EXTERIOR PAINT AND OTHER FINISHES

Surface Types	Oil or Oil-Alkyd Paint	Cement Powder Paint	Exterior Clear Finish	Alumi-num Paint	Wood Stain	Roof Coating	Trim Paint	Porch & Deck Paint	Primer or Under-coater	Metal Prime	Latex House Paint	Water Repellent
Wood Surfaces												
Clapboard	X.			X					X		X.	
Natural Wood Siding & Trim			X		X							
Shutters & Other Trim	X.						X.		X		X.	
Wood Frame Windows	X.			X			X.		X		X.	
Wood Porch Floor								X				
Wood Shingle Roof					X							X
Metal Surfaces												
Aluminum Windows	X.			X			X.			X	X.	
Steel Windows	X.			X.			X.			X	X.	
Metal Roof	X.									X	X.	
Metal Siding	X.			X.			X.			X	X.	
Cooper Surfaces			X									
Galvanized Surfaces	X.			X.			X.			X	X.	
Iron Surfaces	X.			X.			X.			X	X.	
Miscellaneous												
Asbestos Cement	X.								X		X	
Brick	X.	X		X					X		X	
Cement & Cinder Block	X.	X		X					X		X	
Concrete/Masonry Porches and Floors								X			X	
Coal Tar Felt Roof						X						
Stucco	X.	X		X					X		X	

Finish Types

. dot at right of X indicates a primer or sealer may be needed before finishing coat is applied
SOURCE: U.S. Department of Commerce

Repair of your particular finish depends on the bracket it falls into, and that means you must first identify the kind of finish. Putting an interior plastic-based paint on an exterior, enamel base paint will not do anything but cause further and more difficult problems.

Before doing any kind of repair on any kind of painted or finished surface, know the paint you are dealing with. If in doubt, take a chip or sample to the paint store and have it identified.

Particular repairs are listed below by category and type.

Exteriors

There was a time when all exterior painting was enamel—it was the only type strong enough to withstand the weather and sun. Now they have perfectly acceptable exterior plastic-based paints that even look like enamel, and for that reason identifying them is sometimes difficult. Again, take a chip to a paint store for positive ID, and be sure to take the chip from the immediate area of the repair place.

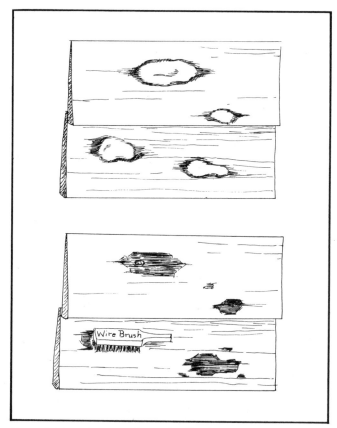

Use wire brush to gently work off paint blisters.

Chips or Peeling

As for actual repair work on exterior paint, you need a wire brush, a small throwaway paint brush and a small can of the right colored paint (matched from the chip). This of course is for small areas, for common repair of a damaged surface. For whole repainting of the outside of a house the work is extensive, and should be considered remodeling rather than repair.* But for the small repair, the work is simple: use the wire brush to thoroughly "scrub" the area to be touched up or repainted. Extend this scrubbing not just to the limits of the damage but out into the good paint around it as well. This will clean the surface and make it slightly abrasive so it will take the paint more tightly. Scrub very hard, and wipe with a dry rag. Then paint in coats. Allow the first one to dry well and stand back ten or fifteen feet to see how it blends in when dry. If it needs to be darker, try another coat. If it does not seem right after the second coat has dried completely, you have a paint mismatch. Either live with it, or take another chip down to the paint store for a second try at the right color. (This happens now and again, especially with red-based colors; they are difficult to match.)

Blistering

Blistering of exterior paint is probably the most common paint repair. If it simply pocks here and there, repair by scrubbing and perhaps sanding lightly; then repaint in spots as per above. Be sure the blisters are not only broken off but that the surrounding surfaces are well taken down, clean, and unflaked.

If blisters are extensive and cover whole sections of wall, repair is likewise extensive and more physically oriented. The wall must be scraped, *each* blister scrubbed and sanded, then the whole wall painted. It is a lot of work and some of it requires working on a ladder.

Fading

Fading of exterior surfaces is another common finish problem. Unfortunately the only true repair is to repaint the whole thing. But before you start measuring the square feet to buy gallons of paint, be certain the wall *is* faded. Quite often a thin patina of silt-dust (usual if you live near a dirt road) will give the

*For a thorough presentation of interior and exterior painting methods, consult *Book of Successful Painting,* by Abel Banov.

Blistering. Large blisters formed and broke under this eave. Cause was moisture reaching the crawl space above the eave, below the sloping roof.

Improper Coating Application Likely to Lead to Blistering. An open invitation to trouble. Blisters will probably form because an oil paint is being applied over condensed moisture, thereby lessening adhesive forces.

Flaking. Incompatible topcoat lifted off this wood after a few months. Primer and topcoat came from different manufacturers.

Handwork for Old Paint. A sharp scraper from your paint or hardware store combined with a little muscle can reduce blisters and flaking surfaces almost level. Sandpaper finishes the leveling process.

impression of fading. Try hosing the house down, then let it dry well. It is worth a try and the "fading" might just disappear.

Note. If you live in a smoggy area, the atmosphere can make the finish look faded. All that debris collects in the cracks and on the flat surfaces. Try warm-to-hot water with a mild detergent and a soft brush or rag; quite often the wash will restore the finish without repainting.

Redwood and Cedar

Redwood and cedar do not require a finish, and are usually just allowed to age. Now and then you

WOOD CLASSIFICATION ACCORDING TO OPENNESS OF PORES

Wood Type	Soft Wood	Hard Wood	Open Pore	Closed Pore	Notes
Ash		X	X		Needs filler
Alder	X			X	Stains well
Aspen		X		X	Paints well
Basswood		X		X	Paints well
Beech		X		X	Varnishes well, paints poorly
Birch		X		X	Paints and varnishes well
Cedar	X			X	Paints and varnishes well
Cherry		X		X	Varnishes well
Chestnut		X	X		Requires filler, paints poorly
Cottonwood		X		X	Paints well
Cypress		X		X	Paints and varnishes well
Elm		X	X		Requires filler, paints poorly
Fir	X			X	Paints poorly
Gum		X		X	Varnishes well
Hemlock	X			X	Paints fairly well
Hickory		X	X		Needs filler
Mahogany		X	X		Needs filler
Maple		X		X	Varnishes well
Oak		X	X		Needs filler
Pine	X			X	Variable
Teak		X	X		Needs filler
Walnut		X	X		Needs filler
Redwood	X				Paints well

Using flat paint brush to paint under siding.

Special flat brush with bristles arranged to paint under siding.

Flat paint brush in use.

will find it has been oiled. If the oil has faded or "sunk" into the wood, repair is simple. Just get some prepared linseed oil and treat the wood to another coat, applying with a brush. Make sure the surface is clean, of course; dust with a broom before applying the oil.

Sometimes the redwood or cedar shake exterior requiring repair will have been bleached. The bleach hastens redwood's natural color change and produces a permanent driftwood gray. One or two coats applied with roller or brush to your repaired section will help match the new redwood to the old.

Other possible finishes to be found on your redwood or shake exterior are stains, either light- or heavy-bodied. They do not obscure the grain; two coats are required.

If no other finish is applied, a water repellant is a good idea. The use of a water repellant will enable you to later change to any other finish without additional preparation. Cuprinol #20, Woodlife, or Pentaseal, will all do a good job.

If for some reason the wood has been painted, be sure that the paint you choose not only matches the original color but is specifically intended for use on exterior redwood. One prime and two finish coats are recommended, and it is a good practice to be wary of the sun when painting—try not to let the sun's rays strike the surface during or immediately after painting.

Plywood

New plywood used for your repair should be given a quick edge-sealing of all panels while they are still in a stack (before installation). This will minimize moisture damage and size variation due to rising and falling humidity.

If panels are not to be painted, such as textured plywood finished with stain, apply a liberal application of water repellant preservative compatible with any finish to be applied later. Horizontal edges, particularly lower drip edges of siding, should be treated. If you want to mask all characteristics other than texture, use an oil, latex emulsion opaque, or highly pigmented stain.

If paint will be used, use a primer and two coats. The best time to paint is during dry, clear weather above 50°F. and below 95°F.

Interiors

Again, the most important requirement for interior repairs is knowledge of the kind of finish being re-

Know Your Wood Grain. Open-grain wood (left) requires filling. Note the broken grain, usually indicative of this type. Close grain wood (right) has more continuous texture, needs no filler.

paired. Take a chip to the local paint outlet; if you cannot decide, let them make the decision for you. After determining the kind of finish, evaluate the damage.

Blistering

With interiors as well as exteriors, a primary problem is blistering—especially in humid rooms (bathrooms) or where heat might be a factor (the kitchen or over the heating store). In these cases, a fan will prevent future blistering.

The repair is the same as for exterior work. "Pop" the blister, scrub it and the surrounding area with a wire brush to insure that it is clean, and match the color by taking a chip from right next to the damaged area. Paint, again, in coats. Allow the first coat to dry well, see how it matches, then add another.

Fading

Fading is, oddly, more of a problem inside the house than outside. The sun will work through a window and leave a very definite color line where it cooks the finish out of the paint. The obvious repair, naturally, is to just repaint the affected wall after making certain that it is not just dirt. Try washing with warm water and mild detergent. But if the faded area is small, say down in the corner of the wall, you might try treating it as a simple small repair. Match the paint by taking a chip from the good area and paint by "feathering" the new paint job into the old. Do it a coat at a time, and let dry well before deciding whether or not you have a good color match.

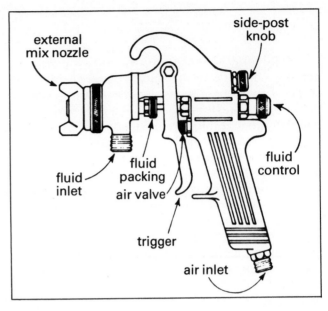

Spray gun.

external mix nozzle

side-post knob

fluid inlet

fluid packing

air valve

trigger

fluid control

air inlet

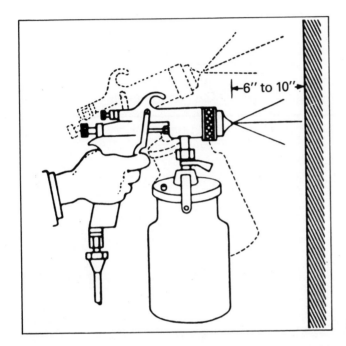

6" to 10"

Positioning of Spray Gun.

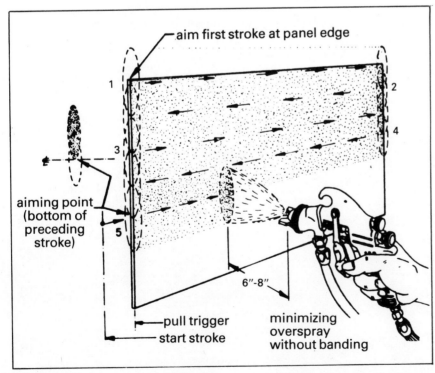

aim first stroke at panel edge

1   2

4

3

aiming point (bottom of preceding stroke)

5

6"-8"

pull trigger
start stroke

minimizing overspray without banding

Spraying Technique for Large Flat Areas. As illustrated, a definite pattern must be followed by the painter if good results are to be achieved. Note also that there is an optimal distance from the spray gun orifice to the work surface.

Yellowing

Yellowing is another problem that seems to happen more indoors than out, usually with off-white colors. The repair is to repaint, but first try washing the wall or ceiling that has yellowed with warm water and detergent. It might remove some of the paint if the original painters did not do a proper job, but that is no great loss since you would have had to repaint anyway. If the yellowing does not wash off, clean well and repaint to match.

Some general things to remember on interior painting: first, make *certain* everything is clean and dry and free of dust; dirt, grease or oil will just negate the whole repair because the new paint will lift off as soon as it has dried. Second, match not just the color, but the application method as well. If the original finish was applied with a brush, then do the repair with a brush. If the original job was done with a roller, then you do the same—although you can use the small roller to cut expenses. Also, match the direc-tion of application as well as method—if the brush strokes were originally vertical, sweeping sideways will stand out like a sore thumb.

Finally, don't hurry. Take your time and do the job properly the first time and there is a chance you will not later have to repair your repair. Hand in hand with doing the job right is the understanding of how paints should be used, and the proper application for the proper use.

Do not try shortcuts that will simply bounce back on you later and cause an even bigger headache. Trying to use an interior latex-base paint for outside purposes to save a dollar just will not work—the paint won't last a week. The same goes for using a very cheap, plastic-base paint in a humid area—like in a shower stall or over the humidifier. The paint will just bubble off inside a month or so and you will have to do it over.

Painting, over all other house repairs, will not tolerate shortcuts.

chapter twelve
siding repairs

From a purely numerical standpoint there are so many kinds of siding, of so many different kinds of materials from aluminum to wood to masonite to plastic—and so many things can go wrong with all of them—that presenting specific problems and repairs could take several books.

Still, here are some general repair tips that can save a great deal of time and money, plus notes on several of the more popularly used forms of siding which can be covered in detail.

Before doing repair on any kind of siding it is good to consider why you need the repair. One good reason is that prompt repair can prevent further deterioration, rust, and later necessary expense. Another reason is the rapid climb in home value, and the fact that buyers often base their offers on what they see when they first come upon a house. You might lose or make several thousand dollars when/if you sell your home merely because of the condition of the siding.

So no matter the kind of siding or the nature of the repair, the quality of work can vastly affect the amount of money you ultimately get for your home. This means you must take your time and do a good job, since it really matters.

Wood Siding

Using wood for siding—whether it be plywood, shingle, or lap siding—is becoming more expensive. The material is common on older homes but some experts predict that in not too many years wood siding will be virtually nonexistent because of its cost. For this reason, special care should be taken in repair.

Actually, the damage siding can sustain and still be repaired is limited to that caused by weather and by accident.

If the wood is raw cedar or redwood the weather will not hurt it, and the only repair necessary is re-

placement of the damaged piece method (covered shortly).

If the siding is painted, see the chapter on "Finishes" for correct paints and application methods, remembering of course to match possibly faded colors correctly.

Lap Siding

Cracks are the most common damage found in lap siding, other than paint fading. Usually a whole long piece cracks and falls away, calling for replacement of a whole board of siding.

This replacement is not as hard as you might think. Using a small crowbar and claw hammer

Remember that lap-siding is vulnerable to dents. Be careful when working with it.

safety first

Uneven ground can be licked when using ladders by the "Ladder Leveler" extension legs shown above in use on brick steps. Made by Alproco Inc. The extension legs have non-skid feet and are adjustable to 9 inches in ¼-inch increments.

U-Shaped aluminum arm at the top of the extension ladder in above photo is called the "Saf-T-Arm" because it holds the ladder away from the vertical surface allowing ample working room. No bending backward necessary. An inexpensive device that bolts on any ladder made by the Fracon Company, Inc.

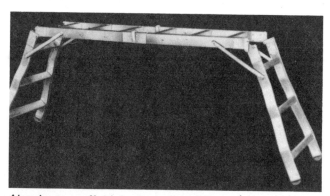

Aluminum scaffold devices of use in re-siding work include the multi-position folding ladder offered by Goldblatt Tool Company (photo above); it can be used in inverted-U form as a low scaffold or in inverted-V form like a stepladder.

At right, the aluminum scaffold planks made by R.D. Werner Company are able to do double-duty as ladders. The metal devices on which they rest are foot-operated jacks that the workman on the scaffold can raise or lower without stepping off the scaffold. They ride up and down a pair of 2x6 posts held in vertical position by roof plates, and are made by the Hoitsma Adjustable Scaffold Bracket Co.

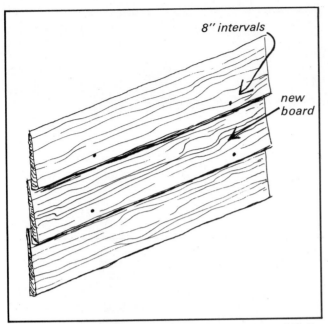

Raise old siding piece; slip in new matching board. Nail through old siding board into top edge of new piece, and through new board into top of board below.

Using a punch, lightly tap nails just under the surface. Then color with a stain or color stick (available in hardware stores).

"raise" the siding board, gently, directly above the board to be replaced and prop it up with scraps of wood.

Now tear out the damaged piece of siding and replace it with a new matching piece from the lumber yard. Nail the new board into underlying studs with 2d or 3d galvanized box nails. Don't worry about studs if underlying sheathing is wood. It is best to nail siding above the top edge of the bottom boards; this permits the siding to expand and contract. Set the bottom nails slightly with a punch, then nail the old top board back down and set those nails slightly too. (See sketch.)

Either paint to match, or let the weather work on it if the wood is raw redwood or cedar.

Tip. Be sure to match new boards to the old ones, and keep them all in line.

Plywood Siding (raw wood)

For major damage, tear out the whole piece of old plywood and match it with a new piece from the lumberyard. Then nail it up. Do not try to piece in a part of a sheet into the hole—it will be nearly impossible to get a decent match and the damage done to the value of the house in looks will far exceed the cost of the plywood. Nail the siding, as in all outside applications, using galvanized nails—with heads—to avoid rust and warpage.

"Lifting" Dents

In both lap siding and plywood, raw or painted, you can repair one kind of ding without jerking the whole board or panel off the wall.

When a small dent occurs—a compression dent and not a tear or gouge, the way a mower might dent when it hits the wall, or a car moving just part of that last inch before stopping—try taking an old damp towel to "iron" the dent out. Just place one thickness of the damp towel over the dent and use your iron, set very hot, to steam the wood back out to its original level; press the iron down hard on the towel so the steam works well into the dent. Quite often this will pull the dent back so that it is difficult to see the damaged place. This is illustrated on the following page.

Be sure to use a grounded, three-wire extension cord when you take the iron outside.

Shingle Siding

The usual problem with shingle or shake siding is a split piece falling out either as a result of age or

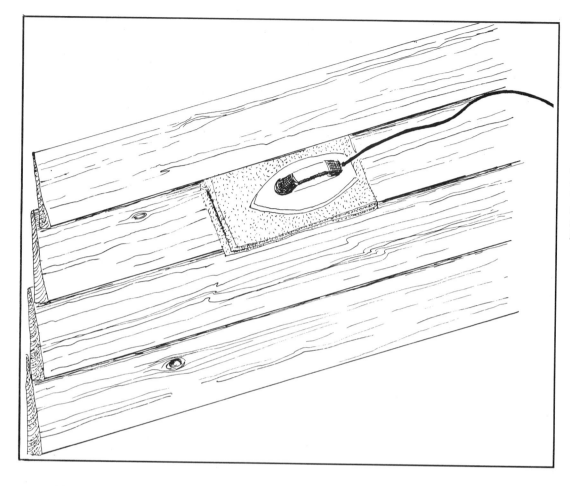

Just have the rag damp, and the iron very hot, and watch carefully to stop as soon as the dent is lifted.

some blow; and the repair is to replace the piece that has fallen out.

Buy a small packet of shingles or shakes from the lumberyard—not a whole square hundred feet, just a packet—and split a piece with a butcher knife or hatchet until it fits the hole.

Then carefully "raise" the shingles above the damaged one and slide the tail or thin portion up under the shingles. Nail as high as possible with galvanized nails (8d or 10d). Do not worry that the shingle seems to stand out—it will quickly weather in.

Note. Usually the full shingle will not fit completely under the row above, but will hit a nail before the bottom or butt of the shingle comes up far enough to align properly with the butts of the shingles already on the wall. Simply cut enough off the thin end to allow the edge to come up to the right place before nailing. It will not leak or look unprofessional.

Metal Siding

As might be expected, the only repair possible with damaged metal siding is complete replacement of the damaged section. Metal siding cannot be steamed smooth or even popped back out the way a body worker repairs the fender on a car.

Replacement methods vary drastically, depending on the kind of metal siding you have and the company who makes it. Complete, specific instructions as to repair and replacement should come with the material when you buy it.

Wear a cheap pair of leather gloves; all metal siding seems to be made of old knives, and small cuts and nicks are the rule.

Remember that all metal, even sheet steel or galvanized steel, has absolutely *zero* resiliency. A hammer dent in wood siding barely shows and can be steamed out easily with your iron. A hammer dent in aluminum siding shows terribly and cannot be fixed properly without replacement, so be extremely careful when you are putting the new material on.

Pull off the damaged piece, being careful not to damage those which are still on the wall. You will note that it was nailed along the top edge, and that the replacement piece likewise has a strip along the top edge for nailing. First, after measuring against

100

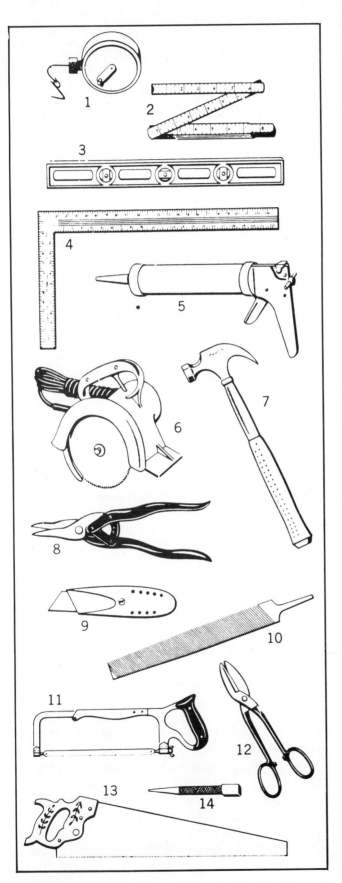

Hand tools for siding application, when using aluminum shown at left, are suggested in the Installation Manual for applications of Alcoa Building Products. Practices and tools used by siding specialists may vary from one area to another. The tools shown are identified as follows: (1) chalk line reel, (2) folding rule, (3) 2 or 4 foot level, (4) carpenter's steel square, (5) caulking gun, (6) electric saw with aluminum cutting blade, (7) claw hammer, (8) double-action aviation snips, (9) utility knife, (10) metal file, (11) fine-tooth hacksaw, (12) tinsnips, (13) conventional cross-cut handsaw, (14) nail set.

siding tools and equipment

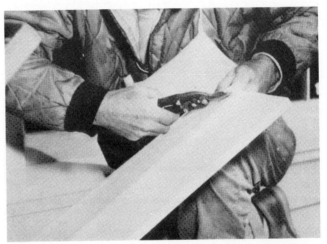

Cut and crimp tools for use with vinyl siding include the precision aviation-type curved-blade snips whose double-acting blades easily follow cutting marks in vinyl (photo above) and a pliers-like hand tool (photo below) called a "Snap-lock Punch." It makes a depression crimp in vinyl cut edges that allow the edge to be inserted into trim strips and locked into position.

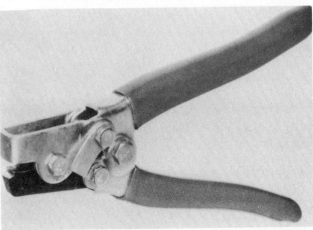

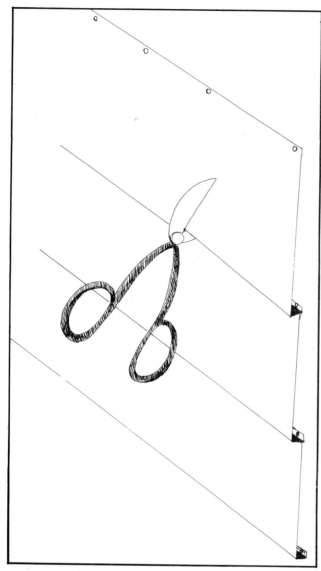

Tinsnips work best on metal siding. Be careful not to dent or bend the new siding piece.

Plastic Siding

Plastic siding, either in lap-wood form or simulated plywood sheets, is much like metal in that severe damage demands replacement of the entire affected piece if it is to look good. And even then colors rarely seem to match because the sun fades the old siding and the new color seems too rich. Often you must paint over it all to overcome this.

On small dents or dings, a great deal of success has been had by filling the damaged spot with fiberglass putty—the premixed material they sell for boat repair. It is necessary to mix it with a catalyst, as per instructions on the can. It hardens fast, but can be tapped and textured with your finger to match the simulated wood grain common with vinyl siding, or it can be sanded smooth to match a smooth surface. Once set it is a simple matter to take a small sample of paint to the local paint store, match it to their chips and touch up the damaged area so that it is almost impossible to tell where the problem was—and it is much cheaper than buying a whole new piece.

Be sure to wear throwaway rubber gloves when working with the putty, and a respirator mask if you intend doing any extensive sanding; the glass fibers are dangerous to breathe.
Note. This fiberglass putty method was tried on the metal siding also, but it did not work well. It adhered at first and seemed adequate for small repair jobs, but over any length of time it came loose and looked cheaply done.

Fiberboard Siding

Made of pressed board to simulate wood lap siding or plywood rough-sawn sheets, repair requires replacement of the whole piece if damage is relatively severe.

Dings, gouges and dents can be fixed with fiberglass putty, being careful to match any simulated wood grain. If the grain does not match the first time, or it does not look pleasing for some reason, you can easily use a screwdriver or chisel to "pop" out the repair job and do it over . . . once it has hardened, naturally.

Paint to match when dry and the repair is finished.
Note. Be certain, even with metal or plastic siding, that on *any* outside application you are using galvanized nails. Anything else will rust and not only look awful but let the job down.

the old piece, use some very good tinsnips or very poor scissors to cut the new piece of siding. Then work the piece in place, up beneath the top piece with the nailer strip against the wall, and over the bottom piece.

Then, awkwardly prying the top piece up, nail with 8d galvanized nails along the strip, up-under, being careful not to miss and to dent the siding. A nail every foot or so will do, and when you are finished nailing just allow the siding to hang down. If it sticks out warp it into place with your hands, until it pushes in with the spring of the metal.

Use a float trowel to plaster smoothly. Then "feather" the new patch mud into the old.

Cement Siding

Stucco

In repairing stucco a great deal depends on the size of the damaged area. For small spots, pull out all the old, dry, and loose stucco around the hole and patch with a handful of thick masonry mortar. Pre-mixed works fine and saves the trouble of mixing sand with cement. Texture to match with your fingers, using a patting motion to "suck" out the cement in little puckers.

Over a large area the work has to be done in two stages. First, after cleaning out all loose and broken particles, use a flat, float-trowel to plaster the entire area smoothly, and bring it out so that it is even with the surrounding wall. Again, use the premix to avoid confusion. Make a thick mixture, adding water slowly as you mix it in a bucket until the cement is about the consistency of loose bread dough—so it will hold a ball if formed in your hand.

Put it on with wide sweeps, and work it well into the mesh-backing already there, "feathering" the patch-mud into the old as in the sketch.

Then let it dry overnight. When it has had a chance to become hard but is still damp—the next day—mix up a batch of fairly runny cement, about like thin cream of wheat. This you apply with a patting motion and an old, coarse sponge. It is easy, and you will find the stucco easy to match after a bit of practice.

Let the patch cure well . . . several days . . . before painting to match.

For smooth-textured patching you mix the cement the same way—following directions on the package—and stop once the smooth patch has been well feathered in. In patching deep holes in concrete walls (for example, on the back of a garage when a car has given it a heavy whack), be sure the hole to be patched is well cleaned and brushed out to insure a good bond. It often helps to dampen the hole before patching; water strengthens cement.

Paint using a good concrete paint. Taking shortcuts with cement is usually fruitless; the paint will just lift off later.

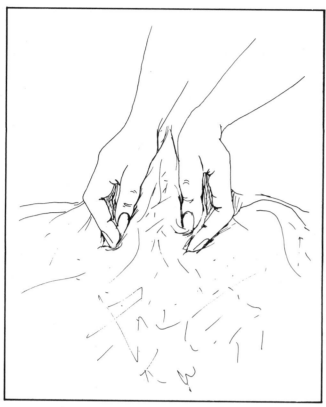

Adobe mud should be slightly runny for final layer, but the base mud should hold a peak when pushed with palm.

Adobe

Adobe mud patching is in a class by itself, but easy and even fun to do.

To patch adobe, first clean the damaged area thoroughly, and let dry. Then mix up some adobe mud, with a touch of cement (about 20 to 1) if you like, from the same area as the original bricks—so the earth-color will match—and apply with your hand or a flat trowel.

To mix adobe base mud, use "tight" earth and add water until mud holds a slight peak when pushed together with your palms. Use this for plastering.

Do not overdo it. If the patch job is deep, apply it in several layers, with the mud again like cream of wheat, to avoid excessive cracking. It is not necessary to mix straw into the plastering mud of adobe; it makes the mud lumpy, difficult to smear well, and hard to work smooth.

For bricks mix up a slightly more runny compound; add straw by the large handful—one for each molded brick. Let bricks cure several days in the sun before using them.

Money Tradeoff

The final thought in this chapter is: you must take time to make the repair look right when you are doing the work yourself. There is no need to hurry or worry, so work slowly. Even if you should make a mistake, don't let it throw you. You can do the job over several times and it will still come out considerably cheaper than if you had called in a contractor.

chapter thirteen
roof repair

Basically, damage to a roof that requires repair comes under one of two categories; it is either dramatic or insidious.

Either your roof is attacked violently by nature, torn apart by wind or hail, or a slow crippling problem will develop that spreads over the entire roof.

In either case repair is mandatory, before a leak can do damage to the interior of the house. Water can wreck drywall the way fire melts wax. Also, in both cases the repair method depends entirely on the material from which the roof is constructed.

Methods are listed below, by material category.

Composition Shingle

The most popular, most widely used, and probably least expensive roof is the asphalt or composition shingle roof. For those unfamiliar with roofing materials, this is the type of shingle that seems to be covered with a gritty substance and is made out of a thick tar-papery material.

Within the spectrum of composition shingles, there are two kinds of application methods—the straight shingle and the interlocking shingle. The straight shingle is simply nailed down, as in the illustration, with the nails (roofing nails) hidden from view by the next row of shingles. The interlocking shingles, which are used in high wind areas, are also nailed down but they have a secondary holding power because two little "tails" on either end lock into the two "tails" on the shingles on either side (see the illustration on page 104).

Strangely, of the two forms of damage mentioned it seems easier to successfully repair the catastrophe. The insidious damage results mostly from age deteriorating the shingles themselves, which lends itself less easily to repair.

Composition shingles are easily repaired by pulling out the damaged one and nailing in the new; curl up the above shingles to take the new one.

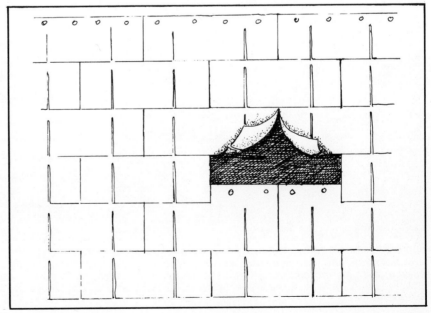

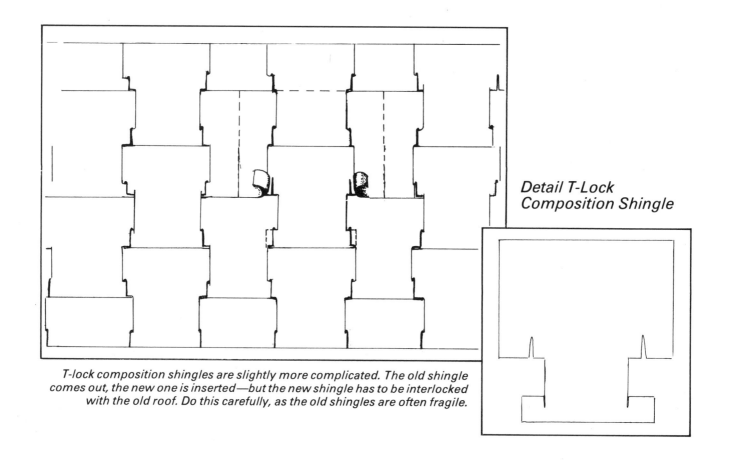

Detail T-Lock
Composition Shingle

T-lock composition shingles are slightly more complicated. The old shingle comes out, the new one is inserted—but the new shingle has to be interlocked with the old roof. Do this carefully, as the old shingles are often fragile.

Footing holds for roof work can be provided simply by temporarily tacking 2x4's in place. Photo above shows new plywood sheathing being applied over old roofing. Footing 2x4's are tacked through wood shingle courses, nail holes filled with caulking after removal. Some roofers use sheet metal straps slipped between shingles to hold the footing 2x4's.

The base upon which new shingles are to be placed needs attention. Nail down or remove protruding roofing nails. Renail split shingles. Replace broken or missing ones. Whether the old roofing is asphalt or wood shingles, get a smooth firm foundation for any new roofing material.

Insidious Roof Problems

As stated, age is the crippler. The sun and weather, over a twenty or thirty year period, truly wreck composition shingles. Leaks begin to show up here and there—trickly, dampening leaks. Repair is elemental, but again, difficult. Buy a small (1 gal.) can of roofing tar, or mastic, and wear soft soled shoes so as not to further damage the roof.

Look for the hole somewhere above the leak spot where it comes throught the roof (usually quite close but not always) and plug it with a dab of tar—just a dab. As the sun cooks, the tar becomes soft; if you put too much on it will actually run down the roof.

If possible, and with great care, lift the shingle and try to get tar underneath as well as on top; work it into the hole gently. It does not take much to stop the leak, and the tar will keep, so do not overdo.

The problem is that when you get that first leak you will probably start to get a lot more of them, assuming the roof is old. You can, of course, keep plugging the holes with tar as they come, but you might want to consider redoing the whole or portions of the roof in the near future.

Catastrophes

The most common sudden damage to composition roofs is from wind: a quick, violent wind will rip out two or three shingles, just enough to leave a bad hole in the roof.

Repair is basic, the damage easily seen and fixed. (See illustration.) You just take one of the damaged shingles to the lumberyard; match it; buy

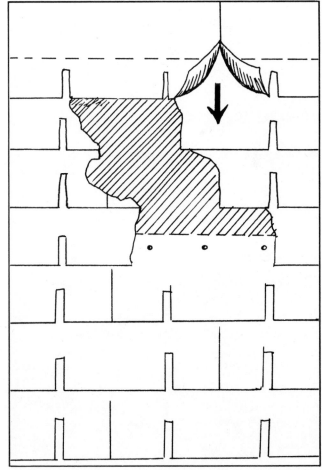

For damage to two or three shingles, leaving a hole, remove old shingles and pull old nails. Work in new shingles, dabbing underside with roofing tar to ensure a good bond.

107

1. The first re-roofing strip along eave will be a 5x36 inch strip, measured and cut so that the 5-inch strip has the black adhesive seal-down striping near the bottom.

2. Balance of the cut strip can then be further trimmed down 2 inches for another 5-inch wide strip without seal-down adhesive, which can be applied later at the ridges.

to re-roof over old asphalt shingles

3. Then position beginning or starter course of the 5-inch wide strips against butt of the second course of old asphalt shingles, with the seal-down striping near the eave edge.

4. Nail starter strip with four nails per strip, placing the nails at a point just below the seal-down adhesive striping.

5. Then place second course of shingle strips trimming the strips down to 10-inch widths. This course is positioned butting to the third course of old shingles.

6. Place third and following courses conventionally, each butting to an old shingle course. This series is from a complete installation set covering Johns-Manville fiberglass shingles.

a packet of shingles (which are handy to have around anyway, just in case) and some roofing nails, and replace the damaged section.

Note. First, gently remove any of the old shingles still remaining, and pull the old nails. Second, as you work in the new shingles (locking them if they are interlocking) it does not hurt to dab them with roofing tar; again, not a lot, but just enough to seal it down. It will insure a good, tight bond and avoid further leaks in the damaged area.

If the damage is massive—if a wind tore off half the roof covering or hail (rarely bad enough to hurt a roof) somehow shredded the entire shingled area, do not try repair on a patch basis. Call your insurance company and recover the whole roof, on a remodeling approach.

tips to handle problem areas...

capping a ridge

Ridge Shingles are single-tab widths cut from shingle strips and applied with same exposure as used with the field shingles. Use one nail each side of the ridge. With hands, carefully pre-bend each ridge shingle. In some areas, suppliers offer pre-cut ridge and hip shingles.

diagonal application

This method makes for easier shingle handling according to expert roofers; this method is preferred, rather than applying full shingle courses across the roof horizontally.

Cementing down of new shingles all around the chimney should be done whether old counter-flashing is used or not. If not, then additional cement caulking should be applied along the joint between shingles and the chimney faces.

Sidewall juncture, the point where a roof surface meets the siding of an upper story, also requires the use of a roofing-felt underlayment strip of flashing plus the cementing down of the adjacent shingles, as indicated in this photo.

making an open valley

Open valley method uses two layers of mineral-surfaced roll roofing and is suitable on jobs where old roofing material has been removed.

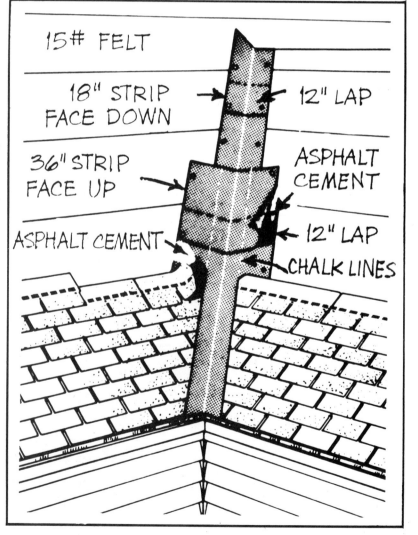

15# FELT

18" STRIP FACE DOWN — 12" LAP

36" STRIP FACE UP — ASPHALT CEMENT

ASPHALT CEMENT — 12" LAP CHALK LINES

Flat Roof—Tar and Gravel

Used on a flat or only slightly pitched roof, the hot-tar-and-gravel surface is probably about the easiest to repair.

Insidious Damage

Generally the place where the water shows up inside will be very close to the hole in the roof surface. There is little traveling because the roof is so flat.

Repair is a matter of dabbing some tar or mastic in and around the hole area, then patting some matching gravel or pea rock (from the driveway) into the still-wet tar or mastic. Use a stick to pat the gravel down because the tar is so sticky; then burn the stick.

Major Damage

The only thing that will wreck a hot tar and gravel roof is probably a hurricane. A new roof put over the old is then about all you can do. Areas or holes up to an inch or so can be patched with the straight-tar-and-gravel method described above.

If a piece a foot or less is ripped out, use tar paper (30# pound felt) and sandwich up the tar and paper, using tar liberally, as illustrated. Cover with matching gravel.

Large holes call for hot patches and/or a new roof; it is not only dangerous (the tar is 600 °F.), but difficult.

Wood Shingle; Cedar Shake

Wood shingle and cedar shake roofs are very much a two-edged sword. On the one hand they make a beautiful and durable roof, tight and warm. On the other, wood shingle or cedar shake is probably the most difficult roof material to repair.

Wood roofs are almost always steeply pitched—otherwise the roof will not shed snow and rain sufficiently to keep the shake or shingle from leaking. The pitch angle not only makes working on the roof difficult and hazardous, but leaks tend to "travel" around.

Because of the steepness of the roof the water might be coming through the shingles up near the peak, coming through the tar paper sheathing halfway down or so and not coming through into the house until it has traveled many feet away from the actual hole.

Insidious Leaks

Start, naturally, where the leak is coming through the main roof into the house. If you are lucky the leak will be right there and you can plug it with a tiny bit of tar or mastic or colored (gray) caulking compound. Just a small amount should be squirted unto the hole, no extra.

Usually your luck is not that good. The leak will be somewhere above the area where it comes through into the house.

The only way to find it is start a thorough search up the roof using a ladder, taking your time and going

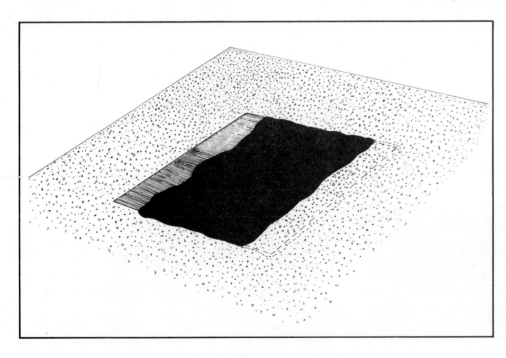

Hot tar and gravel is easily cold-patched. Just remember to wear old clothes and take everything slowly.

To repair cedar shake or shingles, be sure to "roll" them out slightly as in the illustration, so the new shingle goes in easily. Note that the seam between two shingles falls in the central area of the shake below—away from the seam—to avoid leaks.

inch by inch. Just keep looking, and if you cannot find the hole try again until you do see it. Then plug it with a bit of tar or caulking.

The leak *will* show itself, either as an open crack or hole or missing shingle-piece. You must keep at it until you find the leak. If it is a split-out piece insert a replacement split that is the right width (as in the sketch).

Major Damage

Wind, fire, or hail damage—the three causes of major roof problems with wood surfaces— call for completely replacing the damaged shingles or shakes.

Here the work is simple, although physically demanding. It is much like laying up a small new roof.

Just lay up the shingles or shakes as in the sketch, starting at the bottom or eave and working up at the same intervals as the surrounding roof.

When you get to the last row, to facilitate "feeding" the replacement shingles up into the old row above, move across the roof with a claw hammer and loosen the top (next) row of the old undamaged roof, but gently.

Then slide the new shingles in up under the old, nail as high as you can, and tap the old row back down on top of the new row.

Of course it is vital to remember the basic principle of all shingle roofing: stagger the shingles so that a whole shingle always covers the crack between two above to avoid leaks.

Replace shingles on an old wood-shingled roof if there are broken or missing shingles. Simply insert the replacement up under the course above, and nail down.

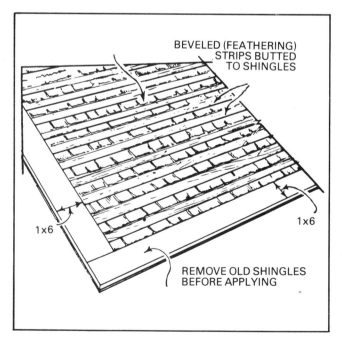

BEVELED (FEATHERING) STRIPS BUTTED TO SHINGLES

1x6

1x6

REMOVE OLD SHINGLES BEFORE APPLYING

Add wood strips to firm up the base to which the reroofing materials will be attached. The drawing on p. 112 indicates new six-inch wide strips along eaves and rakes, since these areas are most likely to show decay. Apply strips so top surface is flush with old roofing. At right, feathered strips butt to old wood shingles. Beveled wood siding boards make good feathering strips.

Metal edging applied along eaves and rakes will provide a proper drip edge and prevent moisture backup under the roofing material. Instruction details on these pages and the drawings have been excerpted from the application manual issued by the Asphalt Roofing Manufacturers Association.

Also, especially important on steeply pitched roofs but a rule that holds true when working in any high area, take everything slowly and carefully. No roof repair is worth a fall and possible severe injury.

Note. On truly steep roofs, as on an A-frame or chalet, repair can be greatly facilitated by renting a set of roof-jacks with which to make a plank-scaffold to stand on. Instructions come with the jacks, but follow directions carefully and exactly.

Special Roofs

There are literally dozens of different specialized roof coverings—from ceramic tube tiles to so-called scientific wonder coverings (generally very risky)—so that we cannot cover each in detail here.

But generally, most of the different roof materials come under the heading of common sense; if you think a repair might work, it probably will work.

Tar, mastic, or closely colored caulking (and instructions for use come with caulking, on the tube) will fix most small leaks on any kind of roof.

In cases of metal roofing, where major damage has been sustained—usually wind ripping off whole pieces—replacement of the whole piece is necessary. Just pry up the "above" section, as shown in the illustration, and insert the new piece, caulking everything liberally.

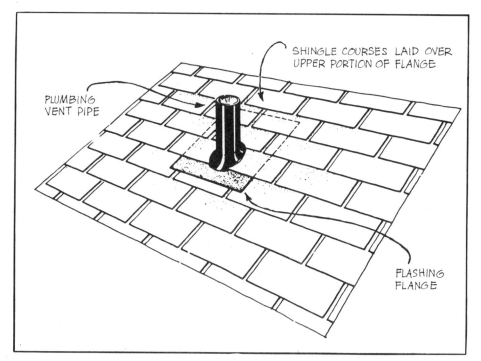

SHINGLE COURSES LAID OVER
UPPER PORTION OF FLANGE

PLUMBING
VENT PIPE

FLASHING
FLANGE

Check flashings at all plumbing stack and vent projections through the roof. Flashing flanges should be interleaved as indicated with the new shingling. If old roofing remains in place, so does the flashing, and the new shingles are cut to fit the projection and cemented down around it.

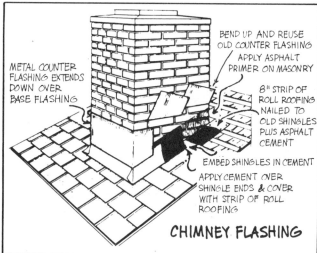

METAL COUNTER
FLASHING EXTENDS
DOWN OVER
BASE FLASHING

BEND UP AND REUSE
OLD COUNTER FLASHING
APPLY ASPHALT
PRIMER ON MASONRY

8" STRIP OF
ROLL ROOFING
NAILED TO
OLD SHINGLES
PLUS ASPHALT
CEMENT

EMBED SHINGLES IN CEMENT

APPLY CEMENT OVER
SHINGLE ENDS & COVER
WITH STRIP OF ROLL
ROOFING

CHIMNEY FLASHING

tips to handle flashings

Chimney flashing when re-roofing can often make use of old counter-flashing when the old material is still serviceable.

Two ways of flashing through-roof projections such as plumbing stacks or ventilators. At far left, the technique when re-roofing over an old roof, new shingles are cut to fit around the stack or vent and cemented down. In near left photo, where old roofing has been removed, the regular flashing flange inter-leaf with shingles is used as though it were a new construction job.

Aluminum foil-faced sealing tape can be a real time-saver in re-roofing for flashing around plumbing and chimney roof projections. At left, the foil-faced sealer, which comes in rolls of varying widths, is pressed into place around the base of a plumbing pipe. At right, a 4-inch strip of the sealing material is pressed into position as base flashing around a stone chimney. Called "Flashband", the material bonds to normal building materials. It is useful for other roof flashings also including such locations as sidewall junctures, antenna bases, skylights and ventilators. Made by Evode Inc.

Cementing down both the flashing and the cut valley shingles, insures a tight valley that will drain well without leaking.

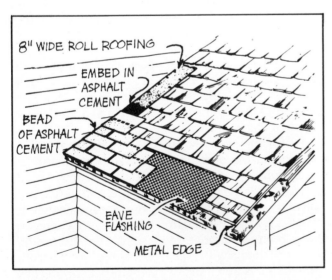

Eave flashing and sidewall flashing with roll roofing cemented down is desirable when new asphalt shingles are being applied over old roofing.

Metal roofing should always be handled with gloves, caulked liberally, nailed with those special metal-roofing nails and never repaired on rainy or windy days.

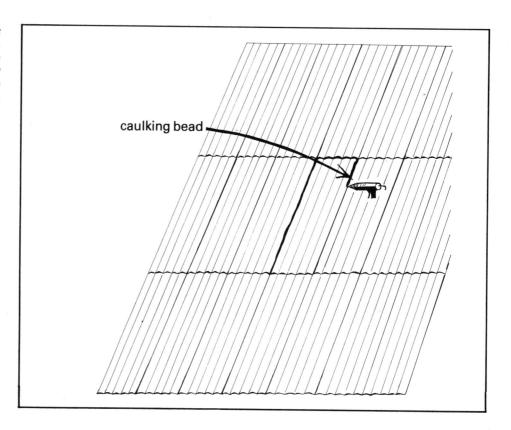

caulking bead

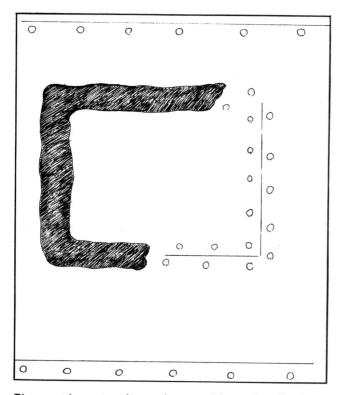

The most important item when repairing roll roofing is to tar the cut-seam liberally when done. Pack it in with a stick, working it wide and long, to make sure the area is leak-proof.

Roll-roofing, which is actually the same as composition or asphalt shingles except that it comes in heavy—about 100 lbs. a roll—rolls, take tar well for small jobs. If a large section is damaged, cut out a square and put in light tar paper to fill the hole. (See sketch.) Then cut a square of the appropriately colored replacement material purchased from the local lumberyard and nail it in with long roofing nails on about four-inch centers. After nailing, smear the tar, really work it into all the seams and over the nails, over everything that might even *think* about leaking. Then when it dries, in a few hours, do it all again and the repair job probably will not leak. Maybe. Also, it will look terrible—like the bottom of an old birchbark canoe—but then roll-roofing isn't chosen for beauty in the first place.

As for the scientific wonder roofing material—use tar, caulking or mastic or epoxy, whatever gets the job done. If damage is severe, an attempt should be made to find a correct replacement material, but to be blunt most of the wonder-roof companies seem to go under at such a rate that finding them when you need a repair is almost impossible. They are doing wonderful things with plastic, of course, but the truth of the matter is that most of the materials coming out seem to break down over time. Sun, weather and wind-driven sand and dirt seem to burn, bake, and beat the guts out of all the new materials. For that reason, it lasts a while and disappears; getting some for replacement is largely a matter of luck.

In the end probably the most important thing to remember about roofs is that a roof that keeps out weather is a good roof. Most or all kinds of roofs can sustain massive amounts of seeming damage—look like they are about to fall off the house—and still keep the weather out. Do not recover a roof just because a contractor going door to door comes by and points out how terrible your roof looks—unless you wanted to anyway, of course. If it is not letting weather through or leaking into the attic, causing very real problems, you need not worry; it might last for several years before it becomes a truly necessary repair problem.

Do not let yourself be railroaded by contractors, even when the problem becomes blatant. When you have got pots and pans catching the drips coming through the ceiling (maybe you don't have to wait that long) still take the time to try repairing it yourself. You can do so without sustaining permanent damage to the house. If your try does not work, then call different contractors, get comparative bids, and make a calm choice.

chapter fourteen

spouts, soffits, and antennae

In a way, soffits are part of the roofing system, but they are also part of the roof-drain system and when the drains go bad they tend to wreck the soffits, where the drains are hooked on.

Drains and Spouts

A good maintenance system is critical in this area of the house. Clean drains, open gutters and downspouts with no leaves or branches fouling them up might mean, literally, ten or fifteen years in the life of the gutter and spout system.

To keep your downspouts from becoming overloaded, use the chart below as a guide for the size needed.

Roof area	Gutter diameter	Downspout diameter
Square feet	*Inches*	*Inches*
100-800	4	3
800-1,000	5	3
1,000-1,400	5	4
1,400-2,000	6	4

When maintenance falls down, so do the drains, and repair is an utter mess. Usually the old drain is nailed onto the last board of the soffit or eave and most often if the drain or gutter is rotted out enough to demand replacement, the board will also be shot. Check it, and if it is bad take a crowbar and (working from a ladder) jerk first the gutter off and then the board, lifting the roofing material (which undoubtedly will not be rotted because it has got a longer life span than drains or wood) out of the way.

Wear long sleeves, goggles, a hard hat, good gloves, and be sure the ladder is secure; then rip and tear. It will be unhappy work but the sooner done the better.

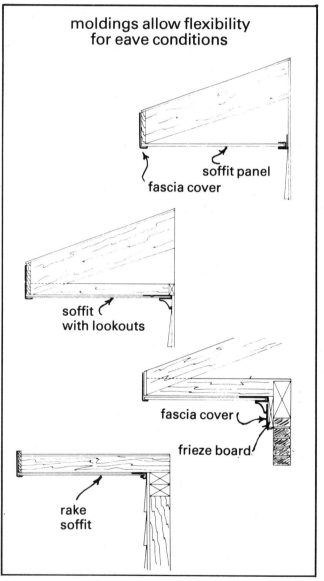

Aluminum products are also available: this drawing indicates varying eave conditions handled by different moldings. These are only a few of the several variations possible. (Art courtesy of Alcan Building Products).

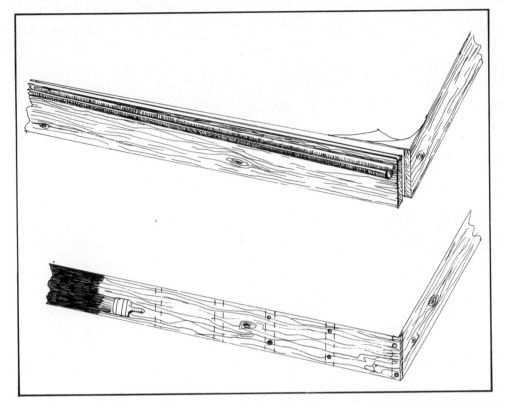

After working the gutter off and then the last soffit board, lift back the roof material (for example, roofing felt) and replace old soffit board with a new one—preferably redwood. Nail with galvanized nails; prime; use oil-based enamel paint. Re-nail gutter to new soffit, or replace with new gutter or trough.

Since the last board of the eave or soffit has been torn out, that is obviously the first item that needs repair. The best choice for replacement is a redwood board, because it resists rot; nail it back on the rafters with galvanized nails and then paint well with a good enamel and proper primers. The idea is to stop future rot before it can get started and before it can work back off the gutters. Anything that will help should be tried.

When the soffit board has been put back in place, painted, and allowed to dry, install the new gutter according to the instructions that come with the gutter. There are several different methods of installation, depending upon the type of gutter purchased, but they are all easy.

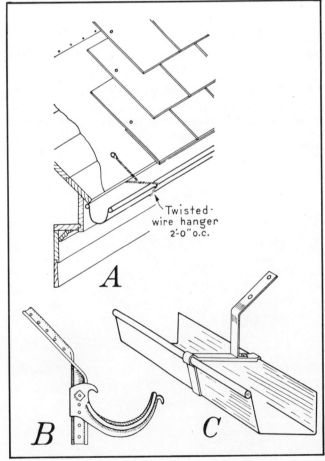

Hanging eaves troughs are a cheaper alternative to built-in gutter downspouts: A, half-round type; B, adjustable hanger; C, box type.

aluminum soffits install easily

Aluminum soffits may offer the simplest route to a complete soffit renovation. Panels must be cut to proper length and slid into position engaging the edge of the previously applied panel. Note that the homeowner is handling panels by edges to avoid fingermarks on the surfaces.

Fasten panels to the old soffit material—a small Bostitch Pneumatic stapler can cut time. The stapler has a slightly projecting nozzle to allow stapling in panel grooves without touching the panel faces.

Staples are driven through soffit panels into edge of old fascia board.

Soffit corners can be handled with a length of double-back-to-back J-channel, stapled into place at a 45 degree angle on a building corner. The doubled J-channel is cut slightly long to allow for mitering cuts, (using aviation-type tinsnips) at each end.

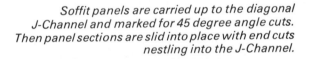
Soffit panels are carried up to the diagonal J-Channel and marked for 45 degree angle cuts. Then panel sections are slid into place with end cuts nestling into the J-Channel.

Here is a front view of soffit installation just before the fascia cover is installed, which will conceal the open ends of the soffit panels. Along this brick wall narrow frieze board has been capped with a custom brake-bent aluminum strip.

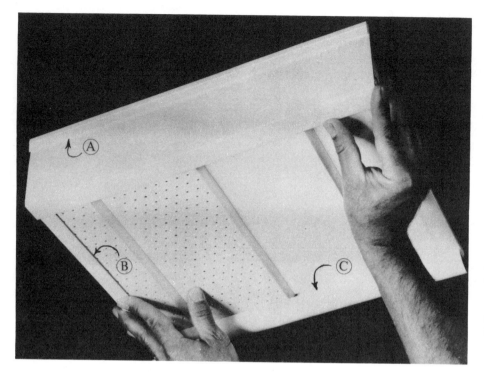

Various parts of a vinyl fascia-soffit system are identified: A, the top edging is an undersill trim designed to hold the top edge of the fascia cover in place; B, a vinyl J-channel trim to finish off the end of the soffit panels; C, quarter-round molding holds the soffit panels firmly while providing a trim. Vinyl materials usually require no unusual tools, and come with instructions that vary with the components provided. (Art courtesy of Bird & Son).

vinyl alternatives

Soffit boards can be replaced with kits: one such is a vinyl fascia-soffit combination that can be adapted to different eave conditions. In A, only the fascia surface is recovered, not the soffit. In B, J-channels are used at the eave and at the house wall, fastened to an existing soffit. New panels are installed below. In C, use is made of an F-channel at eave and the house wall where there was no existing soffit material. New soffit panels in this case are held in place by the channels alone. (Art courtesy of Bird & Son).

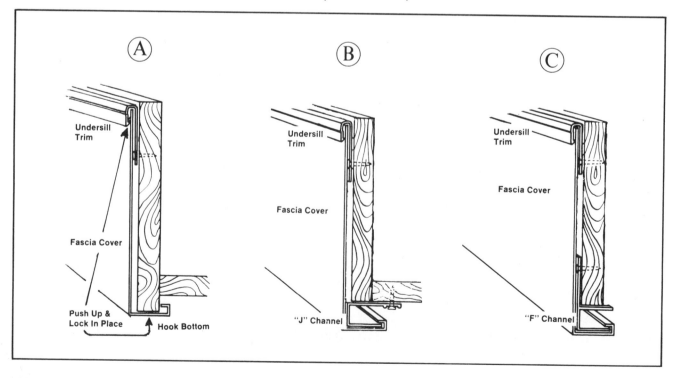

A couple of helpful hints from the past might also help you. First, people used to paint their gutters with tar—just plain old roofing tar—a good coat down the inside. It is a mess to do but once the gutter is in place nobody can see it, and it does offer another coat of very inexpensive protection. Second, in many areas of the country, water shortages have been critical. If you have some old barrels—and this is how they used to get soft water for washing hair—you might wish to store the rainwater for irrigation purposes. Just put the barrel under the spout; it is amazing how fast it will fill.

As for spout repair: if the spouts rot they have to be replaced. This amounts to pulling and replacing brackets.

If your downspouts become plugged with leaves, first try using a hose. From the top just feed a hose going full blast down into the spout, and keep poking until it works through.

If the hose does not work—and it may not if a squirrel has decided to use the spout for winter storage—rent or borrow a plumber's snake and work it up from the bottom while feeding the hose down from the top. Nothing can withstand the two forces working together; move quickly aside when everything lets go.

Erosion

The water draining from a spout often brings an erosion problem which could eventually destroy your yard.

Cement pads are available to put under the drains just for such purposes. Or if you would rather make your own, it is very simple. Get a sack of premix cement for each pad you want, make a wooden frame 10 inches x 24 inches out of 1 x 4 lumber, and fill it with slightly wet cement. Then, wearing rubber gloves, "sculpt" a water pocket and groove down the middle with your hands and let it cure for a couple of days before putting it in place. (See the illustration.) A sheet of galvanized steel will also work.

This galvanized steel gutter was painted before adequate weathering could remove processing chemicals. The only lasting cure is a new gutter.

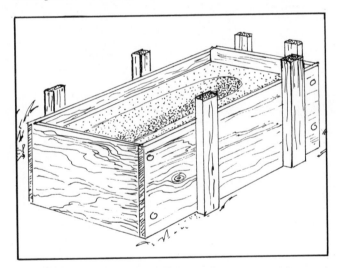

Making your own cement pad to prevent erosion is not hard: build forms for concrete and sculpt a water pocket; be sure to let concrete cure before placing pad beneath water spout.

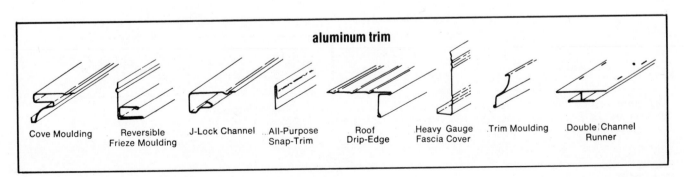

aluminum trim

Cove Moulding   Reversible Frieze Moulding   J-Lock Channel   All-Purpose Snap-Trim   Roof Drip-Edge   Heavy Gauge Fascia Cover   Trim Moulding   Double Channel Runner

Antennae

Television antenna repair almost never varies. You put it up; the wind tears it down; you put it up . . . it is endless, and will go on until they start making them out of something other than thin metal.

Although specific, comprehensive instructions come with all antenna materials, some general hints might be helpful. Most important is to never under any circumstances go up on the roof to work on your television antenna during thunder or rain storms. *Never.* That is crazy—lightning does not give you a second chance. If there is anything even in the vicinity that looks a little like a thunder cloud, leave the antenna alone until it clears up.

It is possible to add a little strength to the antenna. Generally, for roof-mounted antenna systems, they recommend only four and sometimes as few as three guy wires to hold it all down. Ideally, such a system works. But it does not allow for mistakes. With only four wires or three, any one breaking will result in the whole mess coming down.

But if you go to six guy wires on your own initiative, and space them equally around the pole, going out fifteen feet with the wire before tying it down, you might have a chance to ride out the next big wind.

Finally, when you are screwing all those guys into position, put just a tab of caulking on the end of the screws that hold the guy wire down and it will keep leaks from developing.

Then, before coming down, doublecheck everything one more time and align the antenna for your favorite stations.

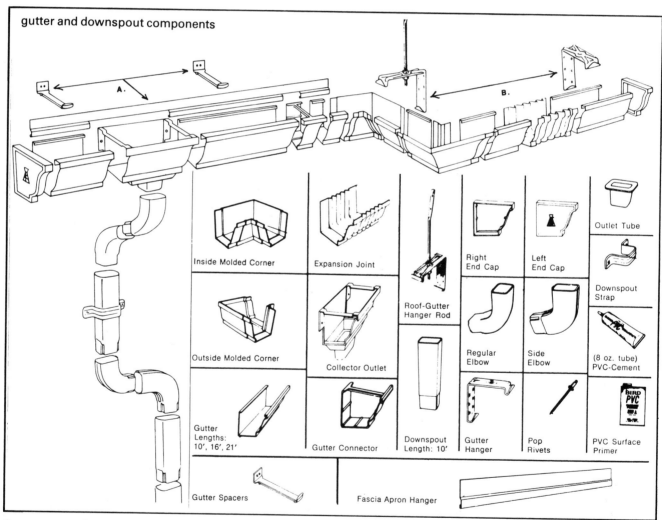

gutter and downspout components

A. B.

Inside Molded Corner
Expansion Joint
Roof-Gutter Hanger Rod
Right End Cap
Left End Cap
Outlet Tube

Outside Molded Corner
Collector Outlet
Regular Elbow
Side Elbow
Downspout Strap

Gutter Lengths: 10', 16', 21'
Gutter Connector
Downspout Length: 10'
Gutter Hanger
Pop Rivets
(8 oz. tube) PVC-Cement

PVC Surface Primer

Gutter Spacers
Fascia Apron Hanger

Components of a solid vinyl downspout system; this brand is produced in white and does not require additional painting. Two methods of hanging are indicated as "A" and "B". (Art courtesy of Bird & Son).

chapter 15

concrete surfaces

All materials deteriorate over time, and concrete is very susceptible. Accidents and wear-and-tear often leave their mark on concrete; freshly cast concrete can be damaged when forms are removed; and, cracks are a common problem.

There are all kinds of repair materials and techniques. The emphasis here will be on those which can be easily handled by the homeowner without special tools or equipment.

The accompanying table lists various types of concrete damage with their suggested repair techniques and materials.

CONCRETE DAMAGE:
Repair Techniques and Repair Materials

Concrete Damage	Repair Technique	Repair Materials
Active cracks	Caulking	Elastic sealants
Dormant cracks	Caulking	Bituminous coatings
	Coatings	Elastic sealants
	Concrete replacement	Epoxies
		Expanding mortars
		High-speed setting materials
		Latex-modified concrete
		Portland cement concrete and mortar
Crazing	Coatings	Epoxies
		Latex-modified concrete
		Linseed oil
		Portland cement mortar
Dusting	Acid etching	Epoxies
	Coatings	Latex-modified concrete
		Linseed oil
		Surface hardeners
Efflorescence	Acid etching	Portland cement mortar
Small holes	Coatings	Dry pack
	Mortar replacement	Epoxies
		High-speed setting materials
		Latex-modified concrete
		Portland cement mortar
Large holes	Coatings	Epoxies
	Concrete replacement	Expanding mortars
		High-speed setting materials
		Latex-modified concrete
		Portland cement concrete and mortar
Popouts	Coatings	Bituminous coatings
		Epoxies
		Latex-modified concrete
Scaling	Coatings	Epoxies
		Latex-modified concrete
		Linseed oil

Adapted from "Concrete Repair Problems: Causes and Cures," *Concrete Construction,* November, 1969.

Identifying the Problem

Here are some definitions of terms to help you recognize the more common types of concrete damage or deterioration.

Cracks. In most cases, cracks should be considered "active," that is, they continue to develop. An unstable subbase can result in uneven settlement and cracking. Incorrect jointing to handle temperature-change effects also results in active cracks.

A "dormant" crack means that it was caused by a factor not expected to reoccur, such as temporary overloading—for example, a car or truck driving over a slab that had not been built for that kind of a load.

Crazing. Crazing cracks are shallow cracks that form a hexagonal pattern. These cracks usually occur shortly after the concrete has hardened. Crazing can be caused by the concrete slab drying out too rapidly—by a rapid loss of moisture from the surface of fresh concrete or by the concrete being placed on a dry subgrade. Other causes could be: too much water in the mix, or excessive finishing. Crazing cracks are usually dormant.

Dusting. Dusting occurs when the surface of the concrete becomes soft and rubs off readily under traffic. Common causes of dusting include: too-wet concrete mixes, excessive finishing, or inadequate curing.

Efflorescence. Efflorescence is the appearance of crystalline salts on a concrete surface. This is caused by water that migrates from the interior of the concrete to the surface as the water evaporates salts are deposited. It does not hurt the concrete, but mars its appearance.

Holes. Whether large or small, if a hole is not cleaned and shaped properly before patching, the patch will probably not hold. It is important to repair holes as soon as possible. Sometimes a "hole" is caused when concrete sticks to the form as it is being stripped (removed). This usually occurs when the forms were not properly coated with oil before concreting. Small holes, called bugholes, may occur along the surface next to a form and are due primarily to entrapped air bubbles. Honeycombing is another so-called hole, but of a different nature. Honeycombing results from the coarse aggregate being placed with an insufficient amount of mortar, because the mix is undersanded, or because poor placing techniques

are followed. To repair these areas you must force mortar into the voids, or remove all loose and poorly bonded material and then replace it all with concrete.

Popouts. Popouts, shallow surface holes, usually occur in slabs. They are caused by expansion of a particle near the concrete surface. Wet or frozen shales, cherts, lignites, and limestones are likely to cause popouts. Some absorbent aggregates that expand when exposed to freezing also cause popouts.

Scaling. Scaling is the sloughing off of thin surface layers of concrete. Scaling can be caused by freezing and thawing of the concrete, use of de-icing salts on concrete which is not air-entrained, poor finishing practices, repeated wetting and drying of the concrete, or chemical attack on the concrete.

Spalling. Spalling is a loosely used term; it usually refers to chunks of concrete that have been broken from the surface by mechanical damage or impact. Spalling is also caused by corrosion of the reinforcing steel.

Repairs

Methods

Most manufacturers furnish specific instructions on the use of their repair products ... be sure to read and to follow them. Listed below are some basic techniques.

Acid etching. Safety precautions must be followed when working with acids. Most acids used for etching concrete cause burns when they come in contact with the skin, and some acids also give off noxious fumes. You should wear protective clothing, gloves, boots, and safety goggles.

Efflorescence can be removed with a 10 percent solution of hydrochloric acid. Sometimes acid etching is used to remove a material from the surface that might impair the bond of a patching material. Usually the concrete is brushed vigorously with a stiff broom with the acid solution. After etching, the acid solution should be thoroughly flushed from the surface as soon as it has ceased foaming.

Caulking. Caulking involves filling fairly narrow openings (cracks) with a plastic compound. Cracks can often be sealed with an elastomeric caulking material.

Coatings. Coatings are materials of liquid or plastic consistency that can be applied directly over concrete. Some coating materials are epoxy resins, bituminous compounds, linseed oil, and silicone preparations.

Concrete replacement. Sometimes conditions are so bad that only complete removal and replacement of the damaged concrete will solve the problem.

Mortar replacement. Mortar replacement is usually confined to shallow holes. The following steps should be followed to achieve a successful repair:

(1) thoroughly clean and shape the cavity;

(2) obtain a good bond between mortar and the old concrete;

(3) vary the consistency of the mortar depending on whether the hole is in a floor or wall;

(4) eliminate or reduce shrinkage;

(5) cure thoroughly.

Sack-rubbing. Sack-rubbing will often improve the appearance of a concrete surface with stains or small bugholes. First spray the concrete with water. Then rub damp mortar over the surface and into the voids with a rubber float or a piece of burlap. Add enough white cement to the mortar to match the color of the surrounding concrete. And, of course, cure the concrete as usual.

A sand finish can be achieved the same way, except that you would rub a creamy, rather than a stiff, mortar over the surface.

Sack-rubbing is most effective when done shortly after forms are stripped. Any large voids should be repaired before sack-rubbing.

Selection of Materials

Many products are available. In all cases, follow the manufacturer's instructions.

For cases where you need water resistance, use a bituminous coating. It can be applied in a thin coat, and is often used to waterproof the exteriors of basement walls.

There are also epoxy-based compounds for many types of concrete repairs. They harden rapidly and resist water. Epoxies can be mixed with fine aggregates to reduce unit cost and make the repair material go further. Epoxy-based compounds are useful where an adhesive is needed to bond plastic concrete to hardened concrete or to bond rigid materials to each other; for patching; or when a thin, strong coating is needed over concrete.

Another popular product is a type of expanding mortar. This was developed to overcome or minimize shrinkage, and can be especially useful in patching.

If you want a speedy set, there are high-speed setting materials that harden and develop strength in a matter of minutes. They come either as admixtures to be added to the mortar or concrete, or as ready-to-use materials requiring only the addition of water. Remember—if the material sets in 5 minutes or less, only a little can be mixed at one time and it must be placed quickly. Read and then carefully follow the manufacturer's instruction.

Scaling

Linseed oil is used when scaling has occurred but without severe enough damage to warrant more extensive repair. The usual solution is a mixture of 50 percent linseed oil and 50 percent mineral or petroleum spirits (by volume). Linseed oil is particularly effective in protecting new concrete when applied before the first freeze and prior to the application of de-icing salt. It penetrates the surface of the concrete to a depth of about $\frac{1}{8}$ inch. The oil inhibits further damage by forming a film that water and salt solutions do not readily penetrate. When used on driveways, it should be reapplied periodically, about every two to four years. Linseed oil does not affect the skid resistance of concrete drives.

Patching

Preparing the Surface to be Patched

Whatever material is used to repair a damaged concrete surface, the patch will only be as strong as the surface to which it is bonded. Make sure the surface should be clean and sound. It must not be contaminated with oil, grease, paint, or mud. The surface can be scrubbed clean with a water-soluble detergent. Heavy deposits of material should be scraped off before scrubbing. Also, there is no point patching over unsound material. Any scaling, crumbling, or loose material must be removed down to clean, hard concrete. Hand picks or chisels can be used to remove unsound material. The depth to which material should be removed from a damaged area will depend on the patching technique and patching compound chosen. If you use portland cement concrete or mortar, the area to be repaired should be removed to a depth of at least 1½ inches. If using a latex-modified mortar, the cut can be less since this compound works well for thinner patches. For most patches, the edges of the hole should be cut roughly square, or even slightly undercut. After chipping out the unsound material, be sure to remove all traces of loose debris and dust.

Portland Cement Patches

Repairs for a concrete slab were covered in Chapter 3. Other repair projects are discussed here.

When using portland cement concrete or mortar as the patching material, the first step is to soak the cleaned bonding surface with water for at least an hour, and preferably overnight, before patching begins.

If the patch is being made in new concrete, work should begin just as soon as possible after removing (stripping) the forms or mold. If the patch is in old concrete, you want to wait after soaking until all surface water has disappeared. The old concrete, just prior to placing the patching mix, should be damp but still slightly absorbent.

Next, a bonding layer is applied to the clean, damp surface. On horizontal surfaces use a grout of portland cement and water mixed to the consistency of thick paint; it should be forced into the base by firm brushing with a semi-stiff bristled brush. On vertical surfaces the bonding layer should be composed of 1 part portland cement and 1 part sand. This mortar should be mixed ½ to 3 hours before use and should be of plastering consistency when applied. Occasional mixing during this period will keep the mortar from stiffening, but do not retemper with water. The bonding layer should be applied to a thickness of about ¼ inch using a stucco brush, but do not apply it too far in advance of the main repair. Otherwise the bonding mortar will dry out.

In general, the mortar or concrete used in the patch should be of the same materials and in the same proportions as that of the base concrete. Since a patch tends to be darker than the surrounding concrete, it is a good idea to substitute white cement for a part of the ordinary gray portland cement used.

For repairing the normal shallow spall, the patching mortar should be built up in layers about ⅜ inches thick. Keep each layer moist for a day or two before placing the next, cross-scratching it to provide a good bonding surface for the next layer. If the patch to be filled is deep, it is often more practical to build a form over the area and to pack concrete behind it.

The patching mix should contain just enough water to give the mix an earth-dry consistency, so that when a pat of mix is squeezed it will "cake," just leaving a trace of moisture in the palm.

On horizontal surfaces, patching concrete should be vigorously hand-tamped in place. On vertical surfaces the concrete should be carefully rodded into place, making sure that the concrete is well compacted and fills corners fully. Then trowel or float the surfaces to the desired finish.

The patch must be thoroughly cured. The patched area should be kept constantly moist for several days and, if practical, curing should continue for as long as a week. If the patch is not carefully cured, it may dry out and shrink away from the old surface.

Epoxy Bonding Agents

Patching with an epoxy-based adhesive is likely to achieve a better bond than patching using a portland cement mortar coating.

When using epoxy adhesives, follow the manufacturer's instructions. The epoxy materials usually come in the form of a two-component system—the base resin and a hardener. Once the two are mixed, the curing process begins with a highly reactive chemical process.

The quantity of bonding agent to be mixed at one time should not be more than can be used up within the pot-life of the agent. This period will be noted by the manufacturer, but generally pot life is about 2 or 3 hours. Pot life means the period during which application is possible. Most bonding agents remain tacky for 1–2 hours after the specified pot life. The new concrete for a patch should be placed anytime during this tacky stage. Tacky set usually begins about ½ hour after application of the epoxy agent, when the free solvents in the mixture have evaporated.

The epoxy bonding material is best applied by stiff bristle brush; this method fills all angles and pores of the surface. Then the stiff mortar is placed and finished.

Be careful when using epoxies; make sure there is adequate ventilation since vapors can irritate the eyes, throat, and lungs. Also important, keep the materials off the skin, since this may lead to severe rashes; always wear gloves. If you spill resin on the skin, wash it off immediately with lots of ordinary soap and water. Do not use a solvent; it will only cause greater skin penetration.

Crack Repair

Crack repair depends on how large the crack is,

its size and depth, and whether it is an active or dormant crack.

If the crack is active, an elastic sealer or caulking material is the best way to seal the crack and still allow movement.

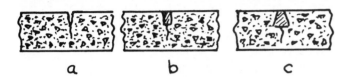

Repairing a wide crack (a), about ¹/₁₆ inch or wider. There are two good ways to cut out the crack for patching: (b) a vertical cut for the edges or (c) an undercut.

The dormant crack can be filled permanently with a patching mortar or compound: portland cement mortar, epoxy mortar, or latex-modified mortar. For a hairline crack, sometimes a grout made of portland cement and water is sufficient. Mix the grout to a thick paste consistency. Force the paste into the crack with a trowel or putty knife, and then smooth level with the concrete surface. As in all repairs, the crack must be cleaned before filling, and the surface should be dampened prior to using the portland cement grout. This kind of patch should be moist cured.

If the crack is more than ¹/₁₆ inch wide it should be chipped away and widened with a hardened-steel chisel. To hold the patching material, the sides of the cut should either be straight or undercut. For small repairs, a prepackaged mortar mix is ideal. These come in packages as small as 5 pounds. A latex-modified mortar or epoxy mortar works extremely well in these situations. If you use a straight portland cement mortar, a typical mix would be 1 part cement to 3 parts sand. Follow the manufacturer's instructions in application. Most repairs call for the old concrete to be well soaked with water and damp at the surface when the mortar patch is applied, and it does not hurt at all to soak the repair area overnight. Once the area has been cleaned thoroughly, force the patching material into the crack, then smooth, and cure.

Repairing Steps and Curbs

Damaged steps and sidewalks are dangerous as well as ugly. Broken corners can be patched with portland cement mortar, but some of today's ready-to-use patching mortars are even easier.

The broken corner should be chiseled and cleaned out. Undercut the edges. Simple formwork may be required to hold the patch if the area is large. At other times the stiff patching mortar will support itself. The patch is tamped and compacted, then floated and troweled. Portland cement mortar requires curing—keep the concrete damp—as do some of the compounds. Wet burlap is a good curing method.

By the way, if the broken corner or piece is still in good shape, it is possible to glue it back in place. Clean the area and use an epoxy or latex mortar (some products are premixed, some you will have to mix). Butter the broken piece with the patching mortar and hold or brace it in place, usually 10 to 15 minutes. After the mortar has stiffened, the excess that has squeezed out can be cleaned off with a trowel or putty knife.

Concrete Stains

Staining may be natural causes or manmade: water run-off can deposit soot or dissolved mineral salts, the family automobile may leak oil on a garage floor. Or someone spills a can of paint. Fortunately you do not have to be either a chemist or a magician to remove most stains. Almost any stain can be removed from recently cured concrete; old, long-neglected stains may require repeated treatments.

To preface a description of specific treatments, here is some general advice on procedures and precautions. The materials and chemicals mentioned below are readily available at drugstores, chemical or laundry supply houses, and possibly at paint or building supply centers. Under normal circumstances the cleaning materials can be used both indoors and outdoors without danger. Naturally, two very basic elementary safety precautions should be taken: (a) wash hands thoroughly after use, and (b) maintain adequate ventilation.

After the stain has been removed it is good practice to wash the area thoroughly with clean water to remove any residue particles of filler, and to be certain that no soluble and possibly detrimental salts remain on the concrete.

If you are not exactly sure what the stain is, it sometimes is better to test a cleaning treatment. Improper materials or techniques could result in spreading a stain over a larger area than originally involved. The best method is to prepare a small trial quantity of the cleaning agent and to apply it at the most inconspicuous point to assess its value. The composition

129

Steps in repairing a broken concrete corner—applicable to steps and curbs—with a prepared patching mortar, Thorite.

a. Cut out all disintegrated concrete until a solid surface is reached.

b. Brush out all loose concrete, chips, and dirt. Dampen area with clean water.

c. While area is still damp, apply a grout coat of patching compound. Work the grout well into the area to be patched.

d. Mix patching compound to a mortar consistency.

e. Force the patching mortar into the area to be repaired, in layers not exceeding 1 inch.

f. Scratch first layer while material is still soft, to assist in maintaining bond between layers.

g. Apply next layer of patching mortar.

h. Overfill the area so that the patch is slightly larger than the surrounding area.

i. Shave off excess until patch conforms to the adjacent area.

j. The patch has been completed and repainted. (Standard Dry Wall Products.)

or strength can then be varied appropriately. This trial-and-error approach applies particularly to the fillers used to form a paste. Different fillers have varying abilities to cling to vertical surfaces.

Also remember that on old concrete, accumulated dirt also disappears with the stains. A limited clean area in a sea of darkened concrete may, in effect, seem just like another stain. Time, wear, and weathering should solve this problem, so that the spot will blend back in with the rest of the concrete.

Treatments

Rust stains. Rust stains on concrete are common. They usually result from weathering of steel or iron attached to or resting on the concrete.

The cleaning materials needed are: sodium citrate crystals, crystals of sodium hydrosulfite, and a paste of whiting and water.

The surface should be soaked with a solution made of 1 part sodium citrate crystals in 6 parts of water. Dip white cloth in this solution and paste it over the stain for 10 to 15 minutes. Or, apply the solution by brush at 5- to 10-minute intervals until the area is thoroughly soaked.

On horizontal surfaces you can sprinkle a thin layer of sodium hydrosulfite crystals, moisten with water, and cover it with a paste of whiting and water.

On vertical surfaces: soak with the sodium citrate solution, place the paste of whiting on a trowel, sprinkle it with sodium hydrosulfite crystals, and plaster the paste over the stained area—making sure the crystals are in contact with the stained area.

Allow the paste to soak in for at least 10 to 20 minutes. Do not leave the paste in place more than one hour, as black staining may result. Remove and flush with clear water. If stain remains, repeat the

131

treatment, but usually a single application is adequate.

Aluminum stains. Aluminum stains usually show up as white deposits on the concrete. The cleaning agent required is a 10 to 20 percent muriatic acid solution. (Remember to observe the label precautions, since muriatic acid can affect eyes, skin and breathing.)

The white deposit may be removed by scrubbing On colored concrete, weaker solutions should be used. Flush with clear water after removal to prevent etching.

Grease stains. Grease normally will not penetrate very far into good dense concrete. Scrape off all excess grease from the surface and scrub with scouring powder, soap, trisodium phosphate, or detergent.

If staining persists, try a solvent. Avoid using free solvents such as gasoline or kerosene, since these only increase the degree of penetration.

Make a paste using a solvent and inert powdered filler. The solvent can be benzene, refined naptha solvent, or a chlorinated hydrocarbon solvent such as trichloroethylene. The filler can be hydrated lime, whiting, or talc. Apply the paste to the stain and do not remove until the paste is thoroughly dry. Repeat the application as often as necessary. Then scrub with strong soap, scouring powder, trisodium phosphate, or detergent (some are specially formulated for use on concrete). Rinse with clear water at end of treatment.

Oil stains. Lubricating or petroleum oil readily penetrates into the concrete surface. With any oil spillage there will be little danger of staining if the free oil is removed promptly. It should be soaked up immediately with an absorbent material such as paper towels or cloth. Wiping should be avoided, as it spreads the stains and drives the oil into the concrete.

Cover the spot with a dry, powdered, absorbent inert material (hydrated lime, whiting, powdered talc or portland cement). Leave it for one day. Repeat this treatment until no more oil is absorbed by the powder. If a stain persists or if oil has been allowed to remain for some time and has penetrated the concrete, other materials will be necessary.

Oils that have solidified should be scraped off as much as possible. Then scrub the area with a clean strong soap, scouring powder, trisodium phosphate or proprietary detergents specially formulated for use on concrete. By the way, a water softener from the laundry room—Calgon—works extremely well.

Wet down the concrete surface and sprinkle on the Calgon (or similar material). Let stand for a little while. Then scrub and flush with water. This will remove most of the free oil. The following treatments can also be used (they are somewhat similar):

1. Make a paste of a suitable solvent, such as benzol, and an inert powdered filler (hydrated lime, whiting, or talc). Apply the paste to the area and allow it to remain in position for at least 1 hour after all solvent has evaporated. Remove and scrub with clear water. Repeat as necessary.

2. Make a poultice with a solution of 5 percent sodium hydroxide (caustic soda). Let dry for 20 to 24 hours, remove, and scrub the surface with clear water. Repeat as necessary.

Paint stains. Dried paint films can be removed satisfactorily by most commercial paint removers. Probably the most effective paint removers are based on methylene dichloride, and are available as liquids, gels, or pastes. Do not use paint strippers that contain acetic acid; these will remove the paint, but may also damage the concrete surface.

The remover should be applied liberally to the area and allowed to penetrate the film for 20 to 30 minutes. Gentle scrubbing will then loosen the paint film and allow it to be peeled or washed off. Wash with water. Any remaining residue can be scrubbed off with scouring powder. Color that has penetrated the surface can be washed out with dilute hydrochloride or phosphoric acid.

This treatment can be applied also to dried enamel, lacquer, or linseed-oil-based varnish. For shellac stains, the paint remover is replaced by alcohol.

Paint removers should not be used on freshly spilled paint or on films less than three days old, since they only tend to increase penetration of the fresh paint into the surface. Absorption with soft cloth or paper towels, followed by vigorous scrubbing, is recommended.

Coffee stains. Coffee stains can be removed by applying cloth saturated in glycerin diluted with four times its volume of water.

Soot. Soot and smoke can be removed by scrubbing the area with ordinary scouring powder. This is followed by an application of sodium hypochlorite (ordinary bleach).

chapter sixteen
if you *must* call the contractor

The premise of this book, as indicated by the title, is how to avoid calling in contractors. And in fully nine cases out of ten there is absolutely no need for calling them in; the homeowner can do the work on his own and get as good a job (often better) as that done by a contractor.

But now and then, for one reason or another, it is unavoidable. This is especially true for senior citizens who perhaps cannot go clambering around on a roof, or people not comfortable working with electrical problems.

For that reason a small chapter devoted to dealing with contractors—home repair contractors, to be specific—seems in order.

Perhaps because of the nature of repair work, since it is always a semi-emergency, or a problem that needs fixing now, home repair contractors seem to be particularly expensive.

There is no norm, of course, no set fee. Generally they charge what the traffic will bear, plus an arm and/or leg; and a job that might cost twenty dollars in one place could easily bring as much as a hundred and fifty in another area. It all depends on the demand and number of contractors in the area.

Be sure the materials and procedures specified for each bid are the same so you will be able to compare accurately.

Because of that, and assuming there is time, shop around. Get several estimates on the repair job you are contemplating and take your time picking the one for the job.

Also, before selecting a repair contractor and after you get the estimate, ask for references. Then check the references. Check and verify everything before you hire and spend money for a job that could go bad on you. But, if the job amounts to less than a hundred dollars, you are unlikely to be able to get bids. In this case it would be better to contact someone you know can be trusted to do the job well and will charge a fair (if not cheapest) price, without bids.

It perhaps goes without saying, but it might bear repeating—get everything in writing. Make the contractor detail the materials, with approximate prices for each, and labor costs, labor amounts, amount of time for the job, date started, and date he estimates completion.

Then check again. Call a few lumberyards and see if the material costs are fair, or even close. It is appalling, but some contractors have been known to double and even triple the amount paid for materials to pick up a few extra bucks. And actually, with material costs exploding upward, doubling a price can be a substantial amount of money.

Another trick tried by some of the more unscrupulous home repair contractors is to go wild and order much more material than needed to complete the job. They then take the surplus home and use it on the next job, passing the expense over to you in the meantime. With an itemized list it is easy to check, and if he is buying four sheets of plywood to cover an area normally covered by one, or getting three gallons of paint instead of one, drop him like a hot rock.

As a final note, because sadly there is no way for knowing ahead of time unless you personally know the contractor what kind of work you will get, call the Better Business Bureau. They will not recommend one contractor over another, but they will tell you which ones to avoid.

The idea of being careful cannot be stressed too much. Literally millions of dollars annually are wasted on completely needless home repair work. Just in the area of heating systems alone there are continual stories of teams of bunko artists going around, talking of vague dangers and unspeakable horrors and selling new heating systems to the unsuspecting when nothing is needed. Some cities have special squads of police just for these crooked home repair contractors, and every fall these squads work steadily to quell the con games.

So be truly cautious if you have to hire a contractor to do the work. Treat the hiring as you would select a doctor; it may cost as much.

133

glossary

Appliances—washers, driers, etc.

Asphalt Tile—square tiles for flooring.

Baseboard Units—Baseboard heating units, either electric or hot water.

Bearings (furnace)—The roller bearings in a blower on the heater, or in a pump on a hot water heating system.

Blower Fan—The heat moving, or air moving part of a forced air heating system, the rotating fan.

Box Beam—A two-by-four and plywood beam structure which allows great strength with light, or comparatively light woods; the plywood is nailed to the sides of the beam, "boxing" it in.

Boiler—The water-heating part (tank) of a hot water or steam heating system.

Breaker (circuit)—Protective switch, in a panel (often in a closet) which "pops" and opens an overloaded circuit.

Butt, Shingle—The heavy, or thick, or bottom end of a shingle.

Carbide Blades—Carbide (hard metal) tipped saw blades for a circular saw—very tough.

Canted Boards—"tipped" or slanted floor boards.

Casing—the "sleeve" of the inside of the well hole going down into the ground—usually metal.

Catalyst—Chemical activator for epoxy or fiberglass resin or putty.

Caulking Compound—putty like mixture, which comes in a tube usually of plastic base, used to plug or "caulk" holes.

Caulking Gun—Small gun-like applicator for using caulking compound tubes.

Ceramic Tiles—Hard, ceramic-clay tiles usually used in baths or kitchens.

Circuit—Electrical term meaning the flow to and from an electrical device—often used to mean wiring.

Circuit Breaker—see Breaker.

Collar Nut—An outside tightening nut, out and around another piece of pipe.

Color Coded—Term used in electrical application; wires are color coded (black is power, white is neutral, green is ground) to prevent mistakes.

Composition Tiles—Asphalt or Vinyl Floor Tiles.

Construction Adhesive—Special glue, which comes in the same tubes as caulking compound, for gluing large areas inexpensively.

Corner Brackets—L-shaped brackets for tightening the corners of doors, especially wooden screen doors.

Coupling—Small section of pipe which slides over two ends of pipe or is threaded to take them and (with galvanized) to hold them together.

Cover Plate—The plastic plate over outlets and switches.

Countersinking screws—To use a cone-shaped drill bit to make a sunken cone to take the head of a countersunk screw.

Crystal—Inexpensive version of plate-like glass; has slight "ripple" effect.

Drain Tube—Water pipe (plastic or metal) which is meant to drain a pressure water area (around footings, as an example).

Drywall Knife—Wide application "knife," not sharp, that looks like a large puttyknife, for working drywall mud.

Drywall Mud—Spackling mud, or drywall cement (either premixed or powder) for repairing drywall.

Drywall Tape—Paper tape used to cover the seams between sheets of drywall—does not have an adhesive back.

Dry Rot—Actually a form of mildew, very advanced, which rots wood in attics.

Ducts—The metal piping (sheetmetal) system for moving hot air around in a hot air heating system.

Emery cloth—Cloth-backed sandpaper.

Eaves—Edge of the roof parallel with the ground.

Enamel—Oil base paint, usually used outside or in high moisture areas (kitchen, bath).

Epoxy—Extremely strong, plastic-based adhesive which must be mixed prior to using.

Feathering—Working the edge of a repair, either paint or drywall mud, back into the existing finish.

Fiberglass Insulation—Insulating material of fiberglass, with paper and/or tinfoil backing, which goes between studs or in rafters.

Fiberglass Putty—A pre-thickened filler made of shredded fiberglass and epoxy resin.

Filter—Air cleaning filter in a hot air—forced air—heating system.

Flame Chamber—Portion of heating system which holds the actual gas flame.

Flat Trowel—Rectangular metal trowel used for working wide areas of mud (drywall) or cement.

Floor Joist—Edge-up board beneath floor which supports the flooring.

Flux—Chemical (acid) cleaning material used in soldering.

Fuse—Small, screw-in container with a wire that melts and opens the circuit if overloaded; usually found in older homes.

Fuse Box—Panel (usually in closet) which holds all the protective fuses for the different circuits in the house.

Galvanized Nails—Nails coated with zinc to stop rusting.

Galvanized Pipe—Plumbing pipe, usually found in older homes, which has been coated with zinc to retard rust and/or corrosion.

Gate Valve—Faucet handle type valve, like the kind on the side of a house for a hose.

Glass Cutter—Small tool, with a tiny hard, cutting wheel, for cutting glass.

Glazing Compound—Putty, for windows, now sometimes made of a plastic base material.

Glazing Points—Small metal points which push into a wooden window frame to hold the glass in place before puttying.

Graphite Lube—Powdered graphite, in a small tube, used for dry-lubrication.

Grout—Filler material, usually dryish mixture of cement, used for filling open cracks and gaps, most often in foundation.

Gutters—Half-pipes along the eaves to channel the water off the roof.

Guy Wires—Wire cables or wires used for support, as in supporting a television antenna on the roof.

Gym-Seal—Varnish-like, *hard* finish for gloss wooden floors; as in typical basketball gyms.

Hand Drywall Saw—Small, single-blade, keyhole type saw for cutting drywall; has very stiff blade and coarse teeth.

Handsaw—Non-electric saw for cutting wood.

Heater Housing (Baseboard)—The metal housing, sheetmetal in construction, around the radiating elements in a baseboard heater.

Heat Sensing Switch—Circuit breaker (or) thermostat.

Hot Water System—Heating system which circulates hot water through pipes to distribute heat.

Jack—Device to lift heavy loads.

Jack, Roof—Device for holding scaffold up on a roof.

Joint Cement—See *drywall mud.*

Lap Siding—Exterior house siding made of boards which overlap.

Latch Assemblies—Door latching mechanisms.

Lath and Plaster—Old method of covering interior walls; found in older homes.

Latex Base Paint—A water base paint, for interior use, dries flat.

Line Surge—A surge of power, more common now than in the past due to energy problems, which causes the voltage in a house to increase slightly.

Linseed Oil—A wood-treatment oil made from flax.

Locksets—Door latch assemblies.

Metal Siding—A house siding, made of sheet aluminum (most often), used in place of lap siding.

Mitered Boards—Boards cut on a mitered (45°) angle.

Nail Punch—Tapered punch for setting finishing nails.

Non-Filling Wood Rasp—Wood rasp with holes through the rasp surface so it won't fill.

Overload—Too many appliances or tools on one circuit.

Outlet—Wall electrical outlet.

Packing—Material inside faucet housing that keeps the housing from seep-leaking.

Paint Scraper—Bladed device for scraping off old paint.

Pilot Hole—Small hole drilled first to allow a bigger bit to be used.

Pipe Rot—Rust-rot of galvanized or metal plumbing pipes, usually found in older homes.

Pipe Wrench—Wrench with backward-sloping teeth to turn smooth pipe.

Plastic Based Paints—See *latex base* paints.

Plywood Siding—Exterior siding, made of sheet plywood, but often made to look like other forms of siding.

Pressed Board—Another name for particle board, a floor sheeting.

Pressure Switching System—The switching system on a well pressure tank, which turns the pump on and off.

Pressure Tank—That portion of a well system, a kind of reservoir, which holds the reserve of water for switching purposes.

Primer—Base paint, undercoating before regular paint on "raw" surfaces.

Propane Torch—(Also Butane torch) A small tank-fed propane torch for soldering and other light heat applications.

P.S.I.—Pounds per Square Inch.

Putty—See *glazing compound*.

Radiation Fins—Small fins on a hot water heating system which radiate the heat; hidden under the baseboard units.

Rafters—Roof support system.

Reset Switch—Mini-circuit breaker located on the appliance or pump; usually a red button.

Ring Washer—Large washer.

Roll Roofing—Composition asphalt roofing in roll form; wide bands of roofing.

Roofing Nails—Big-headed, short, galvanized nails for roof application.

Rotary Saw—Electric handsaw with circular blade.

Sabersaw—Electrical hand-held saw which has an up and down motion of the blade.

Sheetrock—Drywall.

Septic System—Sewage disposal system for the single home.

Shopknife—Small all-around knife with very sharp blade.

Sill Plate—Board that runs around the foundation on which the house sits.

Soffet—Under side of the eaves.

Spackling Paste—Drywall mud.

Stapler—Heavy stapler, gun type, not desk type.

Subfloor—Plywood flooring beneath floor surface.

Sump-Pump—A small pump lowered into shallow water (used most often in basements) to drain it.

Tar—Roofing mastic, a plastic-based tar-like substance.

Torque—Winding energy, associated with a wrench.

Tile Field—The portion of a septic system, a field of porous rocks covered with earth, that spreads the waste liquid out and allows it to sink and purify.

Tracks (Sliding-Door)—Metal tracks above and below a sliding door.

Trowel—Tool for working cement, most often spade-shaped.

Vinyl Sheeting—Imitation wood siding, sometimes in lap form, sometimes panel.

Volts—Unit of electrical work energy, as in 110 Volts or 220 Volts.

manufacturers' addresses

Alcan Building Products
100 Erieview Plaza
Cleveland, OH 44114

Alcoa Building Products
Two Allegheny Center
Pittsburgh, PA 15212

Alproco Inc.
P. O. Box 863
Melbourne, FL 32935

A. O. Smith Company
Consumer Products Division
Box 28
Kankakee, IL 60901

Asphalt Roofing Manufacturers Association
757 Third Ave.
New York, NY 10017

Bird and Son
Washington St.
E. Walpole, MA 02032

Fracon Company, Inc.
690 Wellesley St.
Weston, MA 02192

Goldblatt Tool Company
511 Osage
Kansas City, KS 66110

Hoitsma Adjustable Scaffold Bracket Company
P. O. Box 452
River Street Station
Paterson, NJ 07524

Leviton
59-25 Little Neck Pkwy.
Little Neck, NY 11362

Mapp Products
P. O. Box 105
Springfield, NJ 07081

R. D. Werner Company
P. O. Box 580
Greenville, PA 16125

Standard Dry Wall Products
7800 NW 38th St.
Miami, FL 33166

Index

Other SUCCESSFUL Books

SUCCESSFUL PLANTERS, Orcutt. "Definitive book on container gardening." *Philadelphia Inquirer*. Build a planter, and use it for a room divider, a living wall, a kitchen herb garden, a centerpiece, a table, an aquarium—and don't settle for anything that looks homemade! Along with construction steps, there is advice on the best types of planters for individual plants, how to locate them for best sun and shade, and how to provide the best care to keep plants healthy and beautiful, inside or outside the home. 8½" x 11"; 136 pp; over 200 photos and illustrations. Cloth $12.00. Paper $4.95.

BOOK OF SUCCESSFUL FIREPLACES, 20th ed., Lytle. The expanded, updated edition of the book that has been a standard of the trade for over 50 years—over a million copies sold! Advice is given on selecting from the many types of fireplaces available, on planning and adding fireplaces, on building fires, on constructing and using barbecues. Also includes new material on wood as a fuel, woodburning stoves, and energy savings. 8½" x 11"; 128 pp; over 250 photos and illustrations. $5.95 Paper.

SUCCESSFUL ROOFING & SIDING, Reschke. "This well-illustrated and well-organized book offers many practical ideas for improving a home's exterior." *Library Journal*. Here is full information about dealing with contractors, plus instructions specific enough for the do-it-yourselfer. All topics, from carrying out a structural checkup to supplemental exterior work like dormers, insulation, and gutters, fully covered. Materials to suit all budgets and home styles are reviewed and evaluated. 8½" x 11"; 160 pp; over 300 photos and illustrations. $5.95 Paper. (Main selection Popular Science and McGraw-Hill Book Clubs)

PRACTICAL & DECORATIVE CONCRETE, Wilde. "Spells it all out for you...is good for beginner or talented amateur..." *Detroit Sunday News*. Complete information for the layman on the use of concrete inside or outside the home. The author—Executive Director of the American Concrete Institute—gives instructions for the installation, maintenance, and repair of foundations, walkways, driveways, steps, embankments, fences, tree wells, patios, and also suggests "fun" projects. 8½"x11"; 144 pp; over 150 photos and illustrations. $12.00 Cloth. $4.95 Paper. (Featured alternate, Popular Science and McGraw-Hill Book Clubs)

SUCCESSFUL HOME ADDITIONS, Schram. For homeowners who want more room but would like to avoid the inconvenience and distress of moving, three types of home additions are discussed: garage conversion with carport added; bedroom, bathroom, sauna addition; major home renovation which includes the addition of a second-story master suite and family room. All these remodeling projects have been successfully completed and, from them, step-by-step coverage has been reported of almost all potential operations in adding on to a home. The straightforward presentation of information on materials, methods, and costs, as well as a glossary of terms, enables the homeowner to plan, arrange contracting, or take on some of the work personally in order to cut expenses. 8½"x11"; 144 pp; over 300 photos and illustrations. Cloth $12.00. Paper $5.95.

FINISHING OFF, Galvin. A book for both the new-home owner buying a "bonus space" house, and those who want to make use of previously unused areas of their homes. The author advises which jobs can be handled by the homeowner, and which should be contracted out. Projects include: putting in partitions and doors to create rooms; finishing off floors and walls and ceilings; converting attics and basements; designing kitchens and bathrooms, and installing fixtures and cabinets. Information is given for materials that best suit each job, with specifics on tools, costs, and building procedures. 8½"x11"; 144 pp; over 250 photos and illustrations. Cloth $12.00. Paper $5.95.

SUCCESSFUL FAMILY AND RECREATION ROOMS, Cornell. How to best use already finished rooms or convert spaces such as garage, basement, or attic into family/recreation rooms. Along with basics like lighting, ventilation, plumbing, and traffic patterns, the author discusses "mood setters" (color schemes, fireplaces, bars, etc.) and finishing details (flooring, wall covering, ceilings, built-ins, etc.) A special chapter gives quick ideas for problem areas. 8½"x11"; 144 pp; over 250 photos and diagrams. (Featured alternate for McGraw-Hill Book Clubs.) $12.00 Cloth. $4.95 Paper.

SUCCESSFUL HOME GREENHOUSES, Scheller. Instructions, complete with diagrams, for building all types of greenhouses. Among topics covered are: site location, climate control, drainage, ventilation, use of sun, auxiliary equipment, and maintenance. Charts provide characteristics and requirements of plants and greenhouse layouts are included in appendices. "One of the most completely detailed volumes of advice for those contemplating an investment in a greenhouse." *Publishers Weekly*. 8½"x11"; 136 pp; over 200 photos and diagrams. (Featured alternates of the Popular Science and McGraw-Hill Book Clubs). $12.00 Cloth. $4.95 Paper.

SUCCESSFUL SPACE SAVING AT HOME, Galvin. The conquest of inner space in apartments, whether tiny or ample, and homes, inside and out. Storage and built-in possibilities for all living areas, with a special section of illustrated tips from the professional space planners. 8½"x11"; 128 pp; over 150 B-W and color photographs and illustrations. $12.00 Cloth. $4.95 Paper.

SUCCESSFUL KITCHENS, 2nd ed., Galvin. Updated and revised edition of the book *Workbench* called "A thorough and thoroughly reliable guide to all phases of kitchen design and construction. Special features include how to draw up your own floor plan and cabinet arrangement, plus projects such as installing countertops, dishwashers, cabinets, flooring, lighting, and more. 8½"x11"; 144 pp; over 250 photos and illustrations, incl. color. Cloth $12.00. Paper $5.95.

SUCCESSFUL LIVING ROOMS, Hedden. A collection of projects to beautify and add enjoyment to living and dining areas. The homeowner will be able to build a bar, dramatize lighting, enhance or brighten up an old fireplace, build entertainment centers, and make structural changes. "The suggestions…are imaginative. A generous number of illustrations make the book easy to understand. Directions are concisely written…new ideas, superior presentation." *Library Journal.* 8½"x11"; 152 pp; over 200 illustrations and photos, incl. color. Cloth $12.00. Paper $5.95.

SUCCESSFUL LANDSCAPING, Felice. Tips and techniques on planning and caring for lawns, trees, shrubs, flower and vegetable gardens, and planting areas. "Profusely illustrated…this book can help those looking for advice on improving their home grounds. Thorough details." *Publishers Weekly.* "Comprehensive handbook." *American Institute of Landscape Architects.* Also covers building fences, decks, bird baths and feeders, plus climate-and-planting schedules, and a glossary of terms and chemical products. 8½"x11"; 128 pp; over 200 illustrations including color; $12.00 Cloth. $4.95 Paper.

IMPROVING THE OUTSIDE OF YOUR HOME, Schram. This complete guide to an attractive home exterior at low cost covers every element, from curb to chimney to rear fence. Emphasis is on house facade and attachments, with tips on enhancing natural settings and adding manmade features. Basic information on advantages or disadvantages of materials plus expert instructions make it easy to carry out repairs and improvements that increase the home's value and reduce its maintenance. 8½"x11"; 168 pp; over 250 illustrations including color; $12.00 Cloth. $5.95 Paper.

SUCCESSFUL LOG HOMES, Ritchie. Log homes are becoming increasingly popular—low cost, ease of construction and individuality being their main attractions. This manual tells how to work from scratch whether cutting or buying logs—or how to remodel an existing log structure—or how to build from a prepackaged kit. The author advises on best buys, site selection, evaluation of existing homes, and gives thorough instructions for building and repair. 8½"x11"; 168 pp; more than 200 illustrations including color. $12.00 Cloth. $5.95 Paper.

SUCCESSFUL SMALL FARMS—BUILDING PLANS & METHODS, Leavy. A comprehensive guide that enables the owner of a small farm to plan, construct, add to, or repair buildings at least expense and without disturbing his production. Emphasis is on projects the farmer can handle without a contractor, although advice is given on when and how to hire work out. Includes basics of farmstead layout, livestock housing, environmental controls, storage needs, fencing, building construction and preservation, and special needs. 8½"x11"; 192 pp; over 250 illustrations. $14.00 Cloth. $5.95 Paper.

SUCCESSFUL HOME REPAIR—WHEN *NOT* TO CALL THE CONTRACTOR. Anyone can cope with household repairs or emergencies using this detailed, clearly written book. The author offers tricks of the trade, recommendations on dealing with repair crises, and step-by-step repair instructions, as well as how to set up a preventive maintenance program. 8½"x11"; 144 pp; over 150 illustrations. $12.00 Cloth. $4.95 Paper.

OUTDOOR RECREATION PROJECTS, Bright. Transform you backyard into a relaxation or game area—without enormous expense—using the instructions in this book. There are small-scale projects such as putting greens, hot tubs, or children's play areas, plus more ambitious ventures including tennis courts and skating rinks. Regional differences are considered; recommendations on materials, construction methods are given as are estimated costs. "Will encourage you to build the patio you've always wanted, install a tennis court or boat dock, or construct playground equipment…Bright provides information on choosing tools, selecting lumber, and paving with concrete, brick or stone." *House Beautiful.* (Featured alternate Popular Science and McGraw-Hill Book Clubs). 8½"x11"; 160 pp; over 200 photos and illustrations including color. $12.00 Cloth. $5.95 Paper.

SUCCESSFUL WOOD BOOK—HOW TO CHOOSE, USE, AND FINISH EVERY TYPE OF WOOD, Bard. Here is the primer on wood—how to select it and use it effectively, efficiently, and safely—for all who want to panel a wall, build a house frame, make furniture, refinish a floor, or carry out any other project involving wood inside or outside the home. The author introduces the reader to wood varieties and their properties, describes major wood uses, advises on equipping a home shop, and covers techniques for working with wood including the use of paints and stains. 8½"x11"; 160 pp; over 250 illustrations including color. $12.00 Cloth. $5.95 Paper.

SUCCESSFUL PET HOMES, Mueller. "There are years worth of projects…The text is good and concise—all around, I am most impressed." *Roger Caras, Pets and Wildlife, CBS.* "A thoroughly delightful and helpful book for everyone who loves animals." *Syndicated reviewer, Lisa Oglesby.* Here is a new approach to keeping both pet owners and pets happy by choosing, buying, building functional but inexpensive houses, carriers, feeders, and play structures for dogs, cats, and birds. The concerned pet owner will find useful advice on providing for pet needs with the least wear and tear on the home. 8½"x11"; 116 pp; over 200 photos and illustrations. Cloth $12.00. $4.95 Paper.

HOW TO BUILD YOUR OWN HOME, Reschke. Construction methods and instructions for woodframe ranch, one-and-a-half story, two-story, and split level homes, with specific recommendations for materials and products. 8½"x11"; 336 pages; over 600 photographs, illustrations, and charts. (Main selection for McGraw-Hill's Engineers Book Club and Popular Science Book Club) $14.00 Cloth. $5.95 Paper.

BOOK OF SUCCESSFUL HOME PLANS. Published in cooperation with Home Planners, Inc.; designs by Richard B. Pollman. A collection of 226 outstanding home plans, plus information on standards and clearances as outlined in HUD's *Manual of Acceptable Practices.* 8½"x11";192 pp; over 500 illustrations. $12.00 Cloth. $4.95 Paper.

HOW TO CUT YOUR ENERGY BILLS, Derven and Nichols. A homeowner's guide designed not for just the fix-it person, but for everyone. Instructions on how to save money and fuel in all areas—lighting, appliances, insulation, caulking, and much more. If it's on your utility bill, you'll find it here. 8½"x11"; 136 pp; over 200 photographs and illustrations. $4.95 Paper.

WALL COVERINGS AND DECORATION, Banov. Describes and evaluates different types of papers, fabrics, foils and vinyls, and paneling. Chapters on art selection, principles of design and color. Complete installation instructions for all materials. 8½"x11"; 136 pp; over 150 B-W and color photographs and illustrations. $12.00 Cloth. $4.95 Paper.

BOOK OF SUCCESSFUL PAINTING, Banov. Everything about painting any surface, inside or outside. Includes surface preparation, paint selection and application, problems, and color in decorating. "Before dipping brush into paint, a few hours spent with this authoritative guide could head off disaster." *Publishers Weekly.* 8½"x11"; 114 pp; over 150 B-W and color photographs and illustrations. $12.00 Cloth. $4.95 Paper.

BOOK OF SUCCESSFUL BATHROOMS, Schram. Complete guide to remodeling or decorating a bathroom to suit individual needs and tastes. Materials are recommended that have more than one function, need no periodic refinishing, and fit into different budgets. Complete installation instructions. 8½"x11"; 128 pp; over 200 B-W and color photographs. (Chosen by Interior Design, Woman's How-to, and Popular Science Book Clubs) $12.00 Cloth. $4.95 Paper.

TOTAL HOME PROTECTION, Miller. How to make your home burglarproof, fireproof, accidentproof, termiteproof, windproof, and lightning proof. With specific instructions and product recommendations. 8½"x11"; 124 pp; over 150 photographs and illustrations. (Chosen by McGraw-Hill's Architects Book Club) $12.00 Cloth. $4.95 Paper.

BOOK OF SUCCESSFUL SWIMMING POOLS, Derven and Nichols. Everything the present or would-be pool owner should know, from what kind of pool he can afford and site location, to construction, energy savings, accessories and maintenance and safety. 8½"x11"; over 250 B-W and color photographs and illustrations; 128 pp. $12.00 Cloth. $4.95 Paper.

FINDING & FIXING THE OLDER HOME, Schram. Tells how to check for tell-tale signs of damage when looking for homes and how to appraise and finance them. Points out the particular problems found in older homes, with instructions on how to remedy them. 8½"x11"; 160 pp; over 200 photographs and illustrations. $4.95 Paper.

SUCCESSFUL STUDIOS AND WORK CENTERS, Davidson. How and where to set up work centers at home for the proessional or amateur—for art projects, photography, sewing, woodworking, pottery and jewelry, or home office work. The author covers equipment, floor plans, basic light/plumbing/wiring requirements, and adds interviews with artists, photographers, and other professionals telling how they handled space and work problems. 8½"x11"; 144 pp; over 200 photographs and diagrams. $12.00 Cloth. $4.95 Paper.